The
Connell Guide
to
George Eliot's

———————

Middlemarch

———————

by
Josie Billington

Contents

NOTES

Introduction

When F.R.Leavis, in *The Great Tradition* (1848), situated George Eliot among the "great" novelists of English Literature, and singled out *Middlemarch* as the highest example of its author's "genius", he was rescuing the novel from both scorn and neglect. For the generation of Modernist writers who came after the Victorian period in which George Eliot was writing, *Middlemarch* was one of the "large loose baggy monsters" (as Henry James called the 19th-century realist novel) which were disparaged for their informality and sprawling inclusiveness in a Modernist age concerned with formal unity and impersonal precision.

Yet when *Middlemarch* was first published in 1872, it was recognised as an unprecedented achievement and as marking a new era in the development of the novel. Edith Simcox, later a close friend and personal champion of George Eliot, wrote that *Middlemarch* "marks an epoch in the history of fiction in so far as its incidents are taken from the inner life". One of her shrewdest early reviewers, R.H. Hutton, compared her work to that of her popular contemporary, Anthony Trollope, saying: "He scours a greater surface of modern life but rarely or never the emotions which lie concealed behind. His characters are carved out of the materials of ordinary society;

George Eliot's include many which make ordinary society seem a sort of satire on the life behind."

Today, for fans and detractors alike, *Middlemarch* is synonymous with what we mean by the terms "novel", "realism" and "Victorian", and its power to move modern audiences was demonstrated by the powerful appeal of the BBC dramatisation in 1994. So what makes this novel great even for those who feel cheated or saddened by it? Even such a sensitively enthusiastic reader as the Victorian reviewer Sydney Colvin concluded by wondering how finally "satisfying" such a work can be:

> Is it that a literature, which confronts all the problems of life and the world, and recognises all the springs of action, and all that clogs the springs, and all that comes from their smooth or impeded working, and all the importance of one life for the mass, – is it that such a literature must be like life itself, to leave us sad and hungry?

Yet, for the novel's passionate admirers, Henry James among them, "that supreme sense of the vastness and variety of human life... which it belongs only to the greatest novels to produce" offers its own rich consolations. Perhaps that sentiment is best summed up by the 20th-century novelist Stanley Middleton, who said, if we have no God, we do at least have *Middlemarch*.

A summary of the plot

Prelude:
Reflects on the life of St Theresa of Avila and on
the lives of many women unrecorded by history,
who have shared her potential for heroism
without her opportunities for fulfilment.

Book One: 'Miss Brooke'
We are introduced to the idealistic Dorothea
Brooke, aged 19, and to her younger more down-
to-earth sister Celia, who live with their uncle and
guardian, Mr Brooke, at Tipton Grange. Dorothea,
full of plans for local social reform, is attracted to
Casaubon, more than 30 years her senior, as she
believes with his dedication to learning and
intellectual pursuits he represents "the higher
inward life". Celia finds Mr Casaubon ugly and
dull. Dorothea shocks her family and friends by
accepting Casaubon's proposal of marriage and
visits her new home, Lowick Manor, where she
encounters Will Ladislaw, a younger cousin of
Casaubon's, whom the latter supports financially.
He is painting. As Dorothea and Casaubon marry,
we are introduced to the new Middlemarch
doctor, Tertius Lydgate, and learn of his attraction
to the beautiful and winning Rosamond Vincy.

Book Two: 'Old and Young'

We learn that Lydgate has ambitions beyond those of the average Middlemarch GP. He hopes conscientiously to practise medicine and to shine as an anatomical researcher. The network of relationships widens to include Mr Bulstrode, the puritanical banker, with whom Lydgate hopes to found a new fever hospital under his own medical supervision. Fred Vincy, Rosamond's amiably feckless brother, also depends on Bulstrode's recommendation to obtain funds to pay his gambling debts from wealthy and dying Mr Featherstone. Lydgate becomes friends with mild-mannered clergyman Mr Farebrother, who unselfishly warns Lydgate that voting for him for the new hospital chaplaincy will displease the powerful Bulstrode. Lydgate votes for Bulstrode's choice in the interests of his own career, but is frustrated by the conflicting pressures under which he labours. The close of the book returns to Dorothea, left unhappily alone on her honeymoon in Rome while her husband attends to his studies. She is visited by Will, who is increasingly keen for Dorothea's regard, yet whose presence clearly irks Casaubon. The couple have their first marital quarrel.

Book Three: 'Waiting for Death'

Fred Vincy borrows money from honourable and hard-working Caleb Garth, obliging the family to relinquish their savings and seriously damaging his romantic hopes in respect of his childhood sweetheart, Mary Garth. When Fred falls ill with typhoid fever, Lydgate becomes his doctor and the mutual attraction between Rosamond and Lydgate deepens as their meetings become frequent. Meanwhile, Dorothea returns from Rome, disillusioned with married life and with her limited prospects for doing active good at Lowick. Further tension arises between husband and wife when Will writes to propose a visit to Lowick and Casaubon signals his intention to decline. Casaubon is presently taken seriously ill. Lydgate treats Casaubon, and Mr Brooke replies to Will inviting him to Tipton Grange. The book ends, true to its title, with Mary Garth's vigil on the night of old Featherstone's death when he requests her to burn one of his two wills. She refuses.

Book Four: 'Three Love Problems'

Opens with Featherstone's funeral and news that the will which Mary refused to burn revokes the inheritance left to Fred in the first. Featherstone's estate goes to an unfamiliar mourner, Mr Rigg, whose stepfather, Raffles, now moves into the locality. Rosamond and Lydgate agree an early date for their wedding and Lydgate buys the house of Rosamond's choice though it is beyond his financial means. Meanwhile, Mr Brooke, now running for parliament, has taken over the local

Rufus Sewell as Will Ladislaw in the BBC serialisation of Middlemarch *(1994)*

newspaper, and installed Will Ladisaw as editor. The mutual dislike between Will and Casaubon grows. Will continues to see Dorothea alone and reveals that Casaubon has supported him in reparation for Will's mother's disinheritance by her family when she married against their wishes. Casaubon, increasingly suspicious of Will's intentions, secretly writes to Will insisting he leave the town. Will stays. Farebrother makes his feelings known to Mary Garth, who is moved, but remains loyal to Fred. The book ends with Casaubon learning from Lydgate that he may die at any time.

Book Five: 'The Dead Hand'

Lydgate's new practice and plans for the new hospital meet with opposition, partly because of his association with Bulstrode. Lydgate gets into debt and tension occurs in his marriage as Rosamond fails to understand the importance he attaches to his work. Rosamond becomes pregnant: financial pressure increases. Dorothea feels more than ever her isolation from her husband while Will longs to see her, and is anxious for her good opinion after she finds Will and Rosamond alone together at the Lydgates' home. Casaubon, increasingly mistrusting his wife, asks Dorothea to promise to carry out his wishes should he die, referring, she assumes, to the completion of his work. She asks for time to consider. Next morning, intending to agree to her husband's request, Dorothea finds him dead. Later she discovers Casaubon has added a codicil to his will specifying that she lose all her inheritance should she marry Will. Mr Brooke is humiliated in his election campaign. He suggests Will leave the vicinity; Will refuses. Raffles arrives at Stone Court (old Featherstone's property, now owned by Bulstrode), with knowledge of Bulstrode's first marriage to Will's maternal grandmother. Bulstrode pays him to leave the neighbourhood.

Book Six: 'The Widow and the Wife'

Following the failure of his political hopes, Will

visits Dorothea expressing his intention to depart for London. Strong feelings between the pair are felt, but not expressed. Dorothea mourns the loss of Will's companionship and resolves not to marry again. Fred, now apprentice to Caleb Garth (who has taken management of Lowick estate) jealously learns of Farebrother's feelings for Mary, but Farebrother unselfishly gives Fred and Mary an opportunity to renew their bond. Rosamond disobeys Lydgate's instructions not to go riding while pregnant, has an accident, and loses the baby. Lydgate is dismayed by her wilfulness in relation to their also worsening financial situation, where she resists his suggestions for economy.

As Raffles continues to blackmail Bulstrode, we learn of the banker's past association with a disreputable business which deprived Will's mother (daughter of Bulstrode's first wife) of her inheritance. Bulstrode reveals these facts to Will, offering him a substantial income by way of reparation. Will angrily refuses. Dorothea hears rumours regarding the relationship between Rosamond and Will which she dismisses, while Will learns from Rosamond the import of Casaubon's will. Proudly determined to leave Middlemarch rather than be regarded as an illegitimate fortune-hunter, Will sees Dorothea once more before leaving. At their parting conversation they begin to sense their mutual love.

Book Seven: 'Two Temptations'

As Lydgate's financial problems get worse, he arranges to move to a smaller house. Rosamond cancels the arrangement, to Lydgate's fury, and secretly writes to Lydgate's uncle, Sir Godwin, asking for a loan. The reply of refusal comes direct to Lydgate (now starting to gamble at billiards to the dismay of Farebrother and Fred) who feels humiliated. Bulstrode informs Lydgate he is considering leaving Middlemarch and that Dorothea has offered to take his place as benefactor to the hospital. Bulstrode refuses Lydgate's request for a loan. Raffles arrives near Stone Court, ill, and is helped there by Caleb Garth, who breaks off his business connection with Bulstrode on the strength of Raffles's revelations. Lydgate attends Raffles, specifying the patient must not be given alcohol.

Lydgate returns home to find the bailiffs there and Rosamond distraught. Bulstrode, wishing to influence Lydgate in his favour against possible revelations from Raffles, offers Lydgate the loan he had previously refused. Bulstrode allows a servant to give brandy to Raffles. Raffles dies. As details of Bulstrode's past become common knowledge in Middlemarch, rumour abounds that Bulstrode has bought Lydgate's silence either about his past crimes or his involvement in Raffles's death. Gossip implicates Lydgate too. At a town hall meeting, Bulstrode is forced to resign his position as a leading public figure. When he collapses, Lydgate is compelled to help him from the room, apparently confirming the closeness between the two men.

Dorothea expresses her wish to help Lydgate and is discouraged by Farebrother and Mr Brooke. When Mrs Bulstrode eventually learns the truth of the scandal surrounding her husband, she determines loyally to stand by him. Rosamond is bored and disappointed following Will's departure and jealous of his attachment to Dorothea. When all invitations she sends out for a dinner party are declined, and her father explains to her Lydgate's disgrace, she blames her husband for her shame.

The couple's relationship continues to deteriorate. Dorothea discusses with Lydgate plans for funding the hospital and restoring his reputation, offering to speak on his behalf to Rosamond, and resolving to relieve him of his financial debt to Bulstrode. Lydgate feels unable to continue his involvement with the hospital but is encouraged by Dorothea's faith in him. Calling on Rosamond the following day, she finds the newly-returned Will engaged in intimate conversation with her, and hurriedly leaves the scene in distress. Will, anxious at Dorothea's likely misinterpretation of what she has witnessed, angrily rejects Rosamond, whom Lydgate finds ill on his return. Following an anguished night and powerful emotional reaction, in which she admits to herself the full extent of her love for Will, Dorothea resigns herself to her personal lot and experiences a profound awareness of her place as an individual in a wider world. She resolves to fulfil her promise to Lydgate and visits Rosamond once more, expressing her belief in Lydgate's honour and sympathising with the couple's marital difficulties. In a rare moment of selflessness, Rosamond tells Dorothea of Will's love for her. Rosamond and Lydgate are brought closer in their shared suffering. Will visits Dorothea and they declare their love for each other, Dorothea renouncing her wealth to marry him. When Bulstrode leaves Middlemarch, Fred takes over Stone Court under Caleb Garth's supervision, leaving the way open for Fred and Mary to marry.

Finale:
Summarises later lives of characters. Fred enjoys moderate success as a farmer and a happy marriage with Mary. Lydgate has financially successful medical practice but considers himself a failure and dies at fifty. Dorothea lives happily with Will, who has a career in public life, though is conscious of unfulfilled potential.

What is *Middlemarch* about?

George Eliot called her novels "experiments in life". Here is how the experiment she named *Middlemarch* works.

First, it takes for its setting a historical era undergoing unprecedented change at every level of society and culture. In the first half of the 19th century – the period in which the events of the novel take place – everything suddenly speeded up and the whole scale and shape of ordinary life was transformed. The spectacular growth in the industrial city saw a dramatic rise in population (by 1851 it had doubled in England and Wales since the start of the century and would double again by 1901). The establishment of a national railway network rapidly accelerated migration from rural to urban centres, in the process literally changing the face of the English landscape as well as customary notions of time and distance. By the 1870s, when *Middlemarch* was published, Britain had enjoyed decades of rising prosperity and commercial and manufacturing dominance.

Yet while industry and the railway engine were symbols of the awesome power of technology and the material progress of the nation, they brought colossal social upheaval as older communities, traditions and values were fragmented. Political instability was also a threat, as the powerful middle-classes increasingly demanded representation in government, the working classes agitated for a political voice, and the role of women in a newly constituted democratic society began to come under the public spotlight.   At the same time, religious doubt replaced settled faith as the keynote of the age. Industrial and technological advances encouraged materialist values and ambitions to supplant spiritual ones, while developments in philosophy and the sciences threatened to undermine the very foundations of the Christian religion. The

THE TITLE

Middlemarch: A Study of Provincial Life promises a work concerned not with the fortunes of a single hero and heroine only, but with examining a whole section of society, an entire community. While "study" is suggestive of this intense rigorous analysis, the word also carries (as in artistic production) the sense of "sketch" or (George Eliot's own word for her novels) "experiment". "Provincial" is a critical word here too, marking out not simply a place or a subject-matter, but a perspective (and pejorative attitude?) – that of the (capital) city-dweller for whom the provinces are necessarily an outpost, marginal, distant from the centre. This wider perspective is kept in play throughout the novel. As Gillian Beer has pointed out, it is important to distinguish between *Middlemarch* the book and century's soul had lost its way. As the poet Matthew Arnold put it in 1880, the year of George Eliot's death:

> There is not a creed which is not shaken, not an accredited dogma which is not shown to be questionable, not a received tradition which does not threaten to dissolve.

These happenings were not merely historical to George Eliot (born 1819) but the very medium of her own life. Indeed, as the critic Basil Willey once

---

Middlemarch the town.

The inhabitants of Middlemarch within the book are so confident that Middlemarch is not only in the Midlands but in the Middle of the world; the book's expansiveness creates an effect of size for the town, so that Paris, Rome and London look thin and small by comparison. ... The narrator's business is to remind us of worlds intellectual, aesthetic, spiritual, which do not naturally flourish in the provinces. Not only the individual selves but the collective social self of

Middlemarch is framed and placed.

Whilst Middlemarchers may feel they occupy the Middle of the world, the novel, in its very title, draws attention to their middling mediocrity, their essential typicality and ordinariness. "March" – with its connotations of heroic and purposeful advance and apparent affirmation of the Victorian ideal of middle-class progress – is perhaps ironic in this context. In this novel, any forward march – personal or political – must accept the middle way of compromise.◆

famously said, George Eliot's biography offers a "paradigm" or "graph" of the century's most decided trends. Passionately committed to Evangelical Christianity as an adolescent, she, like so many Victorians, lost her faith under pressure from the exciting and liberating, yet often disconcerting, new ideas of the age. Her first novel, *Adam Bede* (1859) was published in the same year as Charles Darwin's *The Origin of Species,* the definitive expression of evolutionary theory. Suddenly human history did not begin "In the beginning" at the Creation in Genesis, with a divinely-ordered shape and destiny. Instead the human species was the random outcome of a natural struggle for survival and time itself was transformed into something infinitely longer than had been imagined.

George Eliot made her own contribution to the challenging ideas of the period, translating into English the writings of the German philosopher Ludwig Feuerbach. In *The Essence of Christianity*, Feuerbach argued that the virtues of love, charity, mercy, pity which humans had projected onto God were qualities which belonged to humans themselves. Religion, he said, arose as the result of an urgent, imaginative need in humankind to externalise, in the form of a perfect, transcendental being, the very best and highest yearnings and feelings of humanity itself. What was needful now, as Feuerbach (and George Eliot) saw it, was for humans to recognise that the qualities and strengths they had found in God, were really their own. In that way, the human *content* of Christianity could be retained though its trappings – Church, theology, clergy – must be rejected.

Radical unsettlement of *everything* that had been taken for granted in previous generations is the dynamic milieu of *Middlemarch*. The next stage of this creative life-experiment was to people this setting with a vast range of characters who were typical of the movements of the age. Dorothea Booke, the ardently intelligent young woman who frustratedly longs, amid her social privilege, for some wider opportunity in life; Tertius Lydgate the doctor, and ambitious medical reformer; Will Ladislaw, the political radical; Rosamond Vincy, the beautiful and aspiring social climber; Mr Farebrother, the unfulfilled vicar; Mary Garth, the bright and talented young woman, economically forced into a vocation she does not want; Bulstrode, the commercially successful banker; Fred, the penniless gentleman in search of a profession; Casaubon, the scholar whose obsolete research is overtaken by modern thought; Caleb Garth, the farm manager confronted with the impact of the new railway.

Yet for all their representative status, these lives are each presented in their absorbing particularity. It is as if (to borrow one of George

Eliot's many scientific analogies in the novel), the author were subjecting these living individualities (like organisms) to the very same environmental conditions in order painstakingly to test and analyse all possible outcomes. With the most delicately microscopic humane intelligence, the author tracks the rich variousness of the human shapes and responses, in all their subtle and gradual "evolutionary" growth.

Yet it is part of the novel's vision that even this apparently infinite variety will always disclose a connectedness as well. In "Notes on Form in Art", an essay written a little earlier than *Middlemarch* though anticipating its structure, George Eliot wrote that "wholes composed of parts, more and more multiplied and highly differenced" would nevertheless become "more and more absolutely bound together by various conditions of common likeness and dependence".

The essay stems from her Feuerbachian belief in the human species as essentially one large co-dependent family. The interdependence is inscribed in the careful plotting of this novel which unobtrusively interweaves characters' fates so closely that every individual life is ineluctably (for better or worse) a part of the species-life. Yet it is a tribute to the power of *Middlemarch,* and to its loyalty in transcribing the tiny details so often overlooked in life, that for every prepared thread of connection, there are three, four or more unintended ones. The more one reads this novel, the more creative life it seems to give off.

Finally there is one further, and highly distinctive, main character in *Middlemarch* – the voice or language we call "George Eliot". Often regarded as offering a didactic, moralistic and rigidly lofty view from above, in fact George Eliot's voice conscientiously inhabits the precarious space *between* – or the indistinct processes *inside* – characters rather than operating all too knowingly from on top or outside of them. It is not that she is preaching or explaining, but rather as though she hears her characters unconsciously in need of an understanding which they cannot achieve for one another or for themselves. It is the language of rescue work, speaking for the bigger meanings hidden inside the little ones – what she calls, famously, in *Middlemarch*, "the roar on the other side of silence".

Is Dorothea Brooke idealised?

One of the most influential critics of the novel in the 20th century, F. R. Leavis, thought that the one major weakness of this otherwise "great" English novel was the portrayal of the heroine, Dorothea. The narrator's sympathetic identification with Dorothea's passionate idealism – as well as her association with female sainthood (St Theresa and the Virgin Mary) – was a symptom, Leavis claimed, of the author's own "soul-hunger", projected onto her female character. Yet the initial introduction to Dorothea in Chapter One is more subtly critical than indulgent of Dorothea's enthusiasms, deftly exposing them as self-dramatising and self-deluded:

> *She loved the fresh air and the various aspects of the country, and when her eyes and cheeks glowed with mingled pleasures she looked very much like a devotee. Riding was an indulgence which she allowed herself in spite of conscientious qualms; she felt that she enjoyed it in a pagan sensuous way, and always looked forward to renouncing it. (10)*

The narration ironically distances itself from Dorothea's naïve ardour. In fact, the closer the narration gets to Dorothea's own thoughts and language the more subtly powerful its implicit criticism of her idealistic fervour becomes. In the last sentence the voice and language of the narrator mixes almost inseparably with that of the character, ambiguously merging at "she felt", and situating the remainder of the sentence at once inside Dorothea's subjectivism and outside it, as judging witness.

This mode of narration which hovers between first and third person, as if poised between character and narrator (sometimes called *free indirect mode*) is one of 19th-century realism's greatest experiments. The incremental subtlety of its effect is especially apparent in relation to Dorothea, with whose viewpoint the reader sympathetically identifies without ever fully accepting or approving it: "The really delightful marriage must be that where your husband was a sort of father, and could teach you even Hebrew if you wished." The oscillation between emotional closeness and judicious distance is crucial to George Eliot's avowed project as a novelist to present "mixed human beings in such a way as to call forth tolerant judgement, pity and sympathy". One subtle achievement of the author's use of free indirect mode is to suggest that the truest response to a "mixed" reality lies elusively *between* the conventional categories of true and false, right and wrong.

In the equivalent early chapters of Henry

James's own study of what he called "a certain young woman affronting her destiny", *The Portrait of a Lady* (much influenced by George Eliot's work), the tone is often similarly ironic: "Among her contemporaries she passed for a young woman of extreme profundity... Isabel was stoutly determined not to be hollow". (6) Yet James's famed "detachment" from his subject often makes for a less equivocal and more

THE PRELUDE

It is the Prelude which first puts the reader on notice that this is a world living after the end of great things: "spiritual grandeur", "the epic life", the "long-recognisable deed" belong to earlier heroic ages which had not lost "coherent social faith". The narrowness of female opportunity emphasised by the Prelude stands for the conditions which surround, immerse and embroil all the characters who seek to make their mark on the world and who find themselves "packed by the gross and average". But the fact that we know the characters will fail in their ambitions does not "spoil the story" so much as make it acceptable. Without the preparation the Prelude provides for the waste and loss recorded in the novel, the eventual destinies of the characters would have produced a disappointing sense of anti-climax. As it is, we are predisposed to view events as they unfold with a sad sense of irony (the musical analogy is apt, for the Prelude sets the tone as well as the scene) and our expectations are not thwarted – rather fulfilled – by the characters' lesser or middling achievements.◆

determinately sympathetic response to his heroine:

It may be affirmed without delay that Isabel was probably very liable to the sin of self-esteem... Her thoughts were a tangle of vague outlines which had never been corrected by the judgement of people speaking with authority... Few of the men she saw seemed worth [any great vanity of conjecture on the article of possible husbands]. Deep in her soul – it was the deepest thing there – lay a belief that if a certain light should dawn she could give herself completely; but this image, on the whole, was too formidable to be attractive.(6)

The hyperbolic irony of "sin" is directed entirely at the poor judgement of the adult world that has encouraged Isabel's errors, and her depth of soul, whatever its delusions, seems insistently verified and valued here in trenchant contrast to the shallowness of her contemporaries. The tonal differences between the two works are subtle. But they are a clue to the degree to which Isabel Archer's innocence in *The Portrait of a Lady* is in part a tool to expose the corruption of modern society, where Dorothea's thwarted idealism in *Middlemarch* focuses the more religious question of how to live a meaningful life within a world increasingly without direction or purpose.

For Dorothea's egoistic idealism is never simply

proved wrong or mistaken as Isabel Archer's certainly is. Even while Dorothea's naïve expectations of life, and of marriage in particular, are severely chastened in the course of the novel, she never grows out of the "desire" announced in Book One "to make her life greatly effective". The 20th-century critic, Laurence Lerner, famously opposed Leavis's reading by claiming that the

DOROTHEA AND ISABEL ARCHER

In the immediate aftermath of Casaubon's rejection of Dorothea in chapter 42, the separateness of the couple seems to her complete and absolute:

> "What have I done – what am I – that he should treat me so? He never knows what is in my mind – he never cares. What is the use of anything I do? He wishes he had never married me."
>
> She began to hear herself and was checked into stillness. Like one who has lost his way and is weary, she sat and saw as in one glance all the paths of her young hope which she should never find again. And just as clearly in the miserable light she saw her own and her husband's solitude – how they walked apart so that she was obliged to survey him. If he had drawn her towards him, she would never have surveyed him – never have said, "Is he worth living for?" ...
>
> Dorothea sat almost motionless in her meditative struggle, while the evening slowly deepened into night.

Isabel Archer's marriage to Gilbert Osmond in *The Portrait of a Lady* bears a closer resemblance, in many ways, to Gwendolen Harleth's disastrous wedlock with Henleigh Grandcourt in latter's objections to the characterisation of Dorothea were more ethical than artistic: Leavis valued maturity more than idealism – the "Theresa complex" as Lerner called it – where George Eliot's own priorities were arguable the reverse.

The opening chapter of the final book of the novel is a good test-case for this debate, where

George Eliot's later novel *Daniel Deronda* (1876), than to Dorothea's and Casaubon's relationship in *Middlemarch.*But the passage quoted below surely helped inspire James's description of Isabel in *Portrait* sitting "by her dying fire, far into the night, under the spell of recognitions... motionlessly seeing".

> *She had taken all the first steps in the purest confidence, and then she had suddenly found the infinite vista of a multiplied life to be a dark, narrow alley with a dead wall at the end... She had done her best to be just and temperate, to see only the truth... She simply believed he hated her.*

James said of this episode ("obviously the best thing in the book" in his view) that "it was designed to have all the vivacity of incident and all the economy of picture". "In essence, it is but the vigil of a searching criticism; but it throws the action further forward than twenty incidents might have done." (Preface) One can hear behind these intentions George Eliot's own sense of the sheer, near-explosive power that silently and hiddenly resides in inward "events". "The energy that would animate a crime," says the narrator, as Dorothea begins to emerge from her struggle and go out to meet her husband "is not more than is wanted to inspire a resolved submission". (42)◆

Dorothea's "impetuous generosity" towards the disgraced doctor, Lydgate – generally believed to have accepted a bribe from the banker Bulstrode to buy his silence – is pitted against Mr Farebrother's wise maturity. "'Would you not like to be the one person who believed in that man's innocence, if the rest of the world believed him guilty?'" asks Dorothea. "'But my dear Mrs Casaubon,'" counters Mr Farebrother, "smiling gently at her ardour, "'character is not cut in marble – it is not something solid and unalterable. It is something living and changing, and may become diseased as our bodies do.'" (72)

Farebrother's sane common-sense in having only moderate expectation of Lydgate's honour is offered as strong currency here. Mr Farebrother knows all about lowered expectation and compromise – balanced as his life is between the duties and conduct demanded by his vicar's profession, and the economic imperatives which drive him to play cards for money, as well as between the vocation he had wanted, as natural scientist, and the career he has been forced to follow. Throughout the novel, the vicar offers a benign embodiment of adult realism in the face of an attenuated life and represents the "middle way" of equable acceptance of limitation apparently endorsed by the novel's title.

His gentle smile at Dorothea's ardour even recalls the narrator's only delicate ironising of

Dorothea's idealism in Book One; while his pronouncement on character as "not cut in marble" but "living and changing" is often quoted non-contextually as the narrator's own judgement. Farebrother appears to have authority here as the author-narrator's surrogate.

But that mature "narratorial" wisdom seems at best an equivocal virtue when tested against Dorothea's ardent youthful perspective. Where Farebrother – judging Lydgate rather *too much* perhaps by his own sense of life's frustrations – urges Dorothea cautiously to "wait" to know the "truth of [Lydgate's] conduct" before seeking to help him, Dorothea makes an opportunity to see Lydgate and, in one of the most moving scenes in the book, declares her unfailing faith in his good character.

"You have never done anything vile. You would not do anything dishonourable."

It was the first assurance of belief in him that had fallen on Lydgate's ears... The presence of a noble nature, generous in its wishes, ardent in its charity, changes the lights for us... [He] felt that he was recovering his old self in the consciousness that he was with one who believed in it. (76)

Dorothea's trust in Lydgate, when everything else – marriage, career, reputation – has failed, is like a tiny miracle amid mundanity and waste. "She was blind," says the narrator mid-novel "to many things obvious to others, likely to tread in the wrong places; yet her blindness to whatever did not lie in her own pure purpose carried her safely by the side of precipices where vision would have been perilous with fear." (37) Here is a life-experiment in which innocence proves morally safer than maturity. It is an example of how nothing can ever be taken for granted in the realist test of this novel. There is always, as Elizabeth D. Ermarths has put it, an "on the other hand", challenging smug or rigid presuppositions.

Why so many stories?

Book One of *Middlemarch* begins by giving the story the Prelude has promised – that of a woman, a latter-day St Theresa, whose idealistic ambitions for some heroic enterprise are frustrated by the double limitations of her sex and the social conditions of the age. Towards the close of the first Book, however, the focus of the narration suddenly switches from absorbed identification with Dorothea's ardent expectations and hurt disappointments to the fortunes of the interesting newcomer and medical man Mr Lydgate, who will occupy the narrative interest for the next eight chapters. What was background has become foreground, and vice versa.

The swift diminishment of the importance of Dorothea's story is a vindication of the Prelude's pronouncements on the impossibility of exceptional persons or action in the unheroic modern world which is the novel's milieu. As the influential contemporary critic Barbara Hardy has pointed out, Dorothea cannot be a Saint Theresa, nor can there be one single engrossing figure, in a society which can no longer accommodate the "epic life", and where everyone comes to be "shapen after the average and fit to be packed by the gross". (15)

Yet the novel's frequent shift from one centre of interest to another also discloses a multiple and complex reality – a plurality of worlds within one world. Thus, while Middlemarch society speculates on the possibility of an attraction between Dorothea and Lydgate, the latter is "already conscious of being fascinated by a woman strikingly different to Miss Brooke". (11) Lydgate also has his own ambitions: he wants to make Middlemarch itself a medium for scientific discovery and medical reform which will extend far beyond the town's provincial limitation: he means "to do good small work for Middlemarch, and great work for the world". (15) The narrator draws specific attention to this phenomenon when she says, (as the attraction between Lydgate and Rosamond develops): "Poor Lydgate! Or shall I say, poor Rosamond! Each lived in a world of which the other knew nothing." (16)

It is as if *Middlemarch* as a whole seeks to remedy this ordinary human problem of limited vision. For, with each shift of perspective, George Eliot makes her reader do early in the novel what Dorothea learns to do in the course of it – see, that is, not just from one exclusive centre of interest but imaginatively inhabit centres of being opposed to her own. While yet on honeymoon with Mr Casaubon, Dorothea feels "the waking of a presentiment that there might be a sad

"THIS PARTICULAR WEB"

The web imagery woven into the novel's language is a textural counterpart of its complex plotting, with its "stealthy convergence of human lots" and "slow preparation of effects from one life on another". (11). In place of the exclusive history of one human lot (as in the Victorian *Bildungsroman* or novel of development), *Middlemarch* offers a network of overlapping, interwoven human material such that to follow one thread in the story of a single life is necessarily to come upon myriad threads which cross, intercept or frustrate it.

One shorthand way of charting the interpretation of *Middlemarch* over the past half-century is to survey the critical readings of the novel's image of the web. For W. J. Harvey writing in the 1960s, the web was expressive of

consciousness in his life which made as great a
need on his side as on her own".

> *We are all of us born in moral stupidity, taking
> the world as an udder to feed our supreme selves:
> Dorothea had early begun to emerge from that
> stupidity, but yet it had been easier to her to
> imagine how she would devote herself to Mr
> Casaubon, and become wise and strong in his
> strength and wisdom, than to conceive with that
> distinctness which is no longer reflection but
> feeling – an idea wrought back to the directness*

George Eliot's "imperative...
'only connect' ". It signified
"not just her deepest sense of
what life in all its
complications is like, but also
her awareness of the
novelist's duty to give form
and significance to the flux
and chaos of existence." For
Harvey the web was a "key"
to the novel's formal and
philosophical unity. For
Mark Schorer, too, the
"metaphorical system" of the
novel, and the ways in which
characters "share" in it,
demonstrated the thorough
"integration" of George
Eliot's mind and literary
operation, and overcame the
"technical paradox" this
novel presents as a work of
"widely diffused story
materials" with a nonetheless
"powerful effect of unity".
Both critics were writing in
conscious opposition to the
inherited Jamesian objection
to the novel's large, loose
bagginess. Arnold Kettle's
earlier Marxist study of
Middlemarch, however, had
argued that the novel's vision
of "the stealthy convergence
of human lots" figures the
author's conception of
society as a mechanistic,
determining force. She
understands society's power

*of sense like the solidity of objects – that he had
an equivalent centre of self, whence the lights
and shadows must always fall with a certain
difference. (21)*

When Dorothea finds herself at once one of the
two people in the marriage and at the apex of
consciousness between them, she has reached the
level of understanding out of which *Middlemarch*
itself was written. Similarly, when, as here, the
novel rotates the interest from Lydgate back to
Dorothea and her unhappy experience of early

---

but not its dynamism, he said, so that her social vision remains "static" and even at odds with the novel's emphasis upon the power of individual moral choices. Terry Eagleton's later (and still most influential) Marxist reading sees the web imagery as George Eliot's means of imposing a "falsifying" formal unity upon elements within the novels which are ideologically in conflict with one another. Eliot's project is to resolve the contradiction between a belief in social totality and collectivism on the one hand, and the drive for personal self-fulfilment on the other.

J. Hillis Miller's influential reading of *Middlemarch* also interprets the web imagery in the light of the novelist's "enterprise of totalisation". But, rather differently to Eagleton, Miller argues that the novel "elaborately deconstructs" or undermines the ideological assumptions upon which it rests. The "metaphor of vision", in other words, undercuts "the metaphor of the web". "One gets a different kind of totality depending on what metaphorical model is used."◆

marriage, it encourages within the reader an imaginative flexibility of mind and sympathetic feeling analogous to Dorothea's emergence from "moral stupidity".

Like Dorothea, too, the reader is primed to find "equivalence" as much as difference between these stories. The ideal activity enjoined by the book, says Gillian Beer, is that of "making connections". From the closing stages of Book One onwards there is a strong sense of simultaneity in these narrative strands – a sense of the other story carrying on even where it is temporarily out of sight. The novel holds together a multiplicity of separated worlds – Dorothea's, Lydgate's, Casaubon's, Rosamond's, Fred's, Mary's, Mr Bulstrode's, Mrs Bulstrode's – all of which are faithfully preserved in their unique particularity. As we read these narratives forward, we register ironic or affirmative contrasts and comparisons between them, often by the mere dismissal of one character or group and the reappearance of another, and by virtue of their existing together, side by side.

The Book titles offer one clue to the parallels in play. "Young and Old" (Book Two) sweeps into connection Fred Vincy and his uncle Featherstone; Dorothea and Casaubon; Lydgate and Bulstrode; Fred Vincy and Bulstrode; Will and Casaubon. "Waiting for Death" (Book Three) simultaneously nods towards Casaubon and

Dorothea, and Featherstone and Mary who is waiting – literally, since she is nursing the sick man – for the event which will also determine her own future (as Fred's wife or, alternatively, as a teacher or governess). The explicit attention drawn to such correspondences by each book title – "Three Love Problems", "The Widow and the Wife", "Two Temptations" and so on – puts the reader in the habit of seeing more subtle and potentially more far-reaching resemblances.

"George Eliot's intentions are extremely complex," said Henry James. "The mass is for each detail and each detail is for the mass." The sentence brilliantly summarises at once the density of implication contained even in the tiniest particularity of the novel and the subtle inter-relatedness of those particularities.

Why does the narrator have so much to say?

Many of the discursive passages of *Middlemarch* are too clever by half, said Henry James. "The author wishes to say too many things and to say them too well". Yet at the same time James felt that the "intelligence" of George Eliot's imagination was one of the hallmarks of her greatness as a novelist:

> The constant presence of thought, of generalising instinct, of *brain*, in a word, behind her observation, gives the latter its great value and her whole manner its high superiority. It denotes a mind in which imagination is illumined by faculties rarely found in fellowship with it.

The Victorian critic Edward Dowden called that intelligence the author's "second self" – which, "if not the real George Eliot", "writes her books and lives and speaks through them."

Readers of *Middlemarch* often feel that the novel does everything twice over: first a scene is powerfully and minutely depicted, then it is exhaustively analysed and explained. When the contemporary critic, George Steiner, described *Middlemarch* as the most "strenuously narrated" novel in English he had in mind this "personal interference" (as he termed it disparagingly) where "the narrator attempts to persuade us of what should be artistically evident". This common objection to George Eliot's fictional mode is partly a matter of contemporary taste. The tradition of the omniscient or all-knowing author fell out of favour in the last century, when modern readers became reluctant to accept the sort of God-like authority assumed by such a convention. George Eliot's presence in her novels was criticised for its moral "preaching" and for placing the author and reader in a position of wise superiority in relation to characters, always knowing more and better than they do.

Yet George Eliot's interventions are rarely as redundant or merely external to character as these criticisms suggest. So, for example, when the narration turns from "the outside estimates" of Mr Casaubon – "no better than a mummy", "a great bladder for dried peas to rattle in" – to the report of "the man's own consciousness" as his marriage to Dorothea approaches:

Poor Mr Casaubon... was in danger of being saddened by the very conviction that his circumstances were unusually happy: there was nothing external by which he could account for a certain blankness of sensibility which came over him just when his expectant gladness should have been most lively, just when he exchanged the accustomed dullness of his Lowick library for

his visits to the Grange. Here was a weary
experience in which he was as utterly condemned
to loneliness as in the despair which sometimes
threatened him while toiling in the morass of
authorship without seeming nearer to the goal.
And his was that worst loneliness which would
shrink from pity. (10)

The point of the narrator's corrective estimate is
to insist that those aspects of Casaubon which
make him all the less attractive as a husband for
Dorothea – his incapacity for feeling (and sexual
impotence perhaps?) and his lack of an emotionally
rich inner life – make him all the more to be pitied
as a man. This explains why George Eliot as
narrator feels compelled so often in the course of
the novel to speak on Casaubon's behalf – to say
for him what he cannot say for himself.

One morning some weeks after her arrival at
Lowick, Dorothea – but why always Dorothea?
Was her point of view the only possible one with
regard to this marriage? I protest against all our
interest, all our effort at understanding being
given to the young skins that look blooming in
spite of trouble; for these too will get faded, and
will know the older and more eating griefs which
we are helping to neglect. In spite of the blinking
eyes and white moles... and the want of muscular
curve... Mr Casaubon had an intense

consciousness within him and was as spiritually a-hungered as the rest of us.

The narrator intervenes at such times to make up for her character's deficiencies. A person like Casaubon "did not confess to himself, still less could he have breathed to another" his weaknesses and shortcomings. George Eliot *is*, at such times, an added extra because she provides in her novel the voice so often lacking in actual life that speaks up for the failed or inadequate life and saves it, if only at the level of verbal recognition, from being failure merely.

Moreover, George Eliot is never merely speaking *at* the reader. The narrator's impassioned intrusion – "I protest" – momentarily breaks the narrative frame. Paradoxically, by disturbing the illusion that we are witnessing real life, the narration forces us to consider our relation to such figures as Dorothea and Casaubon *in* real life – and here and now, at this present moment of time, when, in our engrossing interest in Dorothea's youthful promise, we are "helping to neglect" the griefs of age. The narrator of *Middlemarch* speaks *to* the reader as a person whom she wishes and expects will bring the narrated story into vital connection with his or her own living experience. The "struggling, erring

creatures" whom George Eliot depicts in the characters of *Middlemarch* as they try to come to terms with their own mistakes, failures, defeats, frustrations, are offered as particularised and moving representations of the Dorotheas, Lydgates and Casaubons who exist outside the novel. If the reader can be made to imagine and feel with the literally unshareable loneliness of the characters in the realist novel, then, the hope – often dimly – is, that fellow-feeling and sympathy can be extended to the real creatures in real life which these characters stand for. "Art," wrote Eliot in "The Natural History of German Life", "is the nearest thing to life; it is a mode of amplifying experience and extending our contact with our fellow-men beyond the bounds of our personal lot".

Moreover, by including the characters in the life of the reader and vice versa, the narrator also speaks *for* the reader. Recounting Dorothea's unhappy honeymoon in Rome, the narrator surmises that the heroine's situation will not "be regarded as tragic":

> *Some discouragement, some faintness of heart at the new real future which replaces the imaginary, is not unusual, and we do not expect people to be deeply moved by what is not unusual. That element of tragedy which lies in the very fact of frequency, has not yet wrought*

itself into the coarse emotion of mankind; and
perhaps our frames could hardly bear much of it.
If we had a keen vision and feeling of all
ordinary human life, it would be like hearing the
grass grow and the squirrel's heart beat, and we
should die of that roar which lies on the other
side of silence. As it is, the quickest of us walk
about well wadded with stupidity. (20)

Such language establishes a community of experience between writer, reader and character, embracing the reader in the narrator's understanding and the narrator in the human limitation ("stupidity") she thus expounds. In thus situating the narrating and reading mind within a syntax of community ("we"), the prose opens up a transactional, meditative-emotional space on the borderline between writer and reader, novel and ordinary life. Rather than simply preaching, George Eliot's language evokes a sort of collaborative consciousness in which the recognition of limitation can amount to something other than limitation merely – something more like sensitive moral expansion.

What are people looking for in Middlemarch?

The central ambition of the intellectual work which first attracts Dorothea to Casaubon is the discovery of "the Key to all Mythologies". (5) What lies behind Casaubon's research is a belief "that all the mythical systems or erratic mythical fragments in the world were corruptions of a tradition originally revealed". (1) The multiplicity and diversity of custom and legend stem, so his theory goes, from a common origin and single tradition or truth. Casaubon's scholarly enterprise is paralleled most closely by Lydgate's scientific search for a unitary source in his anatomical investigations: "What was the primitive tissue?", "the common basis" (15) of all anatomical structures adapted to special bodily functions, the key that will explain the workings of the human organism?

Yet the effort thus to penetrate or to see beyond a multiplicity of meanings or systems to some single authority which generates and explains them is not the exclusive habit of the novel's thinkers and scientists but a characteristic of all central characters. Lydgate's search for the very origins of life is a bold biological version of Dorothea's own desire for a principle of unity to make sense of her own life, the larger life around it and the relation between the two: the "provinces of masculine knowledge" which Mr Casaubon represents to her seem "a standing-ground from which all truth could be seen more truly" (7); "her usual eagerness" is "for a binding theory which could bring her own life and doctrine into strict connection with that amazing past, and give the remotest sources of knowledge some bearing on her actions". (10) All of these examples in turn recall Will Ladislaw's habit of seeing hidden, original wholes from visible fragments: "He confessed that Rome had given him quite a new sense of history as a whole; the fragments stimulated his imagination and made him constructive." (22)

The all-pervasive search for a "key" reflects a general trend in Victorian intellectual life: a Darwinian preoccupation with tracing, observing or creating links between the past and the present. "In the Victorian period," Gillian Beer comments, in her study of the relationship between the novel and evolutionary theory, "the Romantic search for the 'One Life' had been set back in time and become the search for Origins." Yet the search for a key in *Middlemarch* is also a symptom of the absence of "coherent social faith and order" which, the Prelude announces, is the surrounding context and condition of the lives and events depicted in the novel. The quest for unity is part of the individual compulsion – variously and repeatedly demonstrated in the novel – to create a coherent and comprehensive world-view in the absence of a divinely or socially given one. This desire to make sense of oneself and one's place in a fallen world connects the fallacious coherence of Casaubon's mythological and Lydgate's anatomical systems not only to Bulstrode's deviously self-serving divine scheme on the one hand – "In his closest meditations the life-long habit of Mr Bulstrode's mind clad his egoistic terrors in doctrinal references to superhuman ends" (53) – but also to Mrs Cadwallader's

THE TIMING OF THE NOVEL

What seems to have attracted George Eliot to the late 1920s in which the novel is set is that this was a period in which so many areas of national life were undergoing reform. The novel partly chronicles the political events which led to the passing of the 1832 Reform Bill which decisively shifted political power and governmental influence away from the aristocracy by granting representation rights to the middle-class. George Eliot's notes for her novel show she extensively researched not only the stages in the passing of the reform bill but the medical controversies, practices and discoveries of the 1820s and 1830s. Historical reform at all levels is the subject and medium of this novel. Moreover, these were the years which ushered in the subsequent period of far-reaching and often tumultuous social, economic innocently comic and outmoded aristocratic scheme on the other: "She believed as unquestionably in birth and no-birth as she did in game and vermin." (6)

Casaubon's and Lydgate's endeavours are also, of course, two of the novel's most spectacular failures. As Will Ladislaw is all too glad to explain to Dorothea, Casaubon's researches are both futile and obsolete. Lydgate's noble purpose, as medical pioneer bent on revolutionising treatment, issues in mere worldly success as a wealthy physician and in premature death. Does this mean that the

and political change through which the author and many of her readers had lived. It is as if George Eliot were turning back to the originating moments in history which had shaped the contemporary world of her own day, as if seeking the origins of the strong currents that had modified her own contemporary social and political environment. There were specific reasons for doing so in the late 1860s and early 1870s. For 1867 had seen the passing of the Second Reform Bill (which further extended the franchise and caused alarm among certain sectors of Victorian society). George Eliot was thus writing *Middlemarch* in the aftermath of one period of parliamentary change, the passing of the 1867 Reform Act, and looking back to pre-Victorian times, to the confused and not dissimilar events preceding the Great Reform Act of 1832.

The fact that the time of the novel's composition is not only the historical product of, but also comparable to, the period which the novel covers does seem to be a key aspect of the effect the novel means novel itself has no belief in the kind of "binding theory" which its characters so zealously pursue?

Certainly, the lesson both of the novel's web-like structure and dizzying overlap of perspective, as well as of its frequent scientific analogies, is that the relations of cause and effect are irreducibly multiple:

> *Even with a microscope directed on a water-drop we find ourselves making interpretations which turn out to be rather coarse; for whereas under a weak lens you may seem to see a creature*

to produce on the reader. The parallel has an especially material effect on the novel's sense of closure. At one level, the Finale of the novel places the characters and their world in a historically superseded past, even as it depicts them marching positively into the future. Yet what Gillian Beer has called the "double time" created by George Eliot within the novel – "the 'now' of herself and her first readers and the 'now-then' of the late 1820s" – encourages her contemporary readers to see the ambitions of their own age in relation to the failures or muted successes recorded in the Finale. Precisely at the point where the novel seems to be suggesting that these lives are a closed book, irrevocably past, therefore, the novel is also bringing them into resonant connection with the present, by implicitly suggesting the continuance of their concerns into the late nineteenth century. What looks like closure proves to be its opposite, denying finality in a post-heroic age for such problems in respect of reform that Dorothea, Lydgate, Ladislaw and others variously represent.◆

*exhibiting an active voracity into which other
smaller creatures actively play as if they were so
many animated tax-pennies, a stronger lens
reveals to you certain tiniest hairlets which make
vortices for these victims... will show a play of
minute causes. (6)*

The example of Lydgate's failed ambition is a good
test case here. The simple, crude or "coarse"
explanation for his failure might be his mistake
in marrying Rosamond. Yet even that colossal
error of judgement, at the decisive moment
when they become engaged, involves, when
viewed microscopically, his strengths as much
as his weaknesses.

*At this moment she was as natural as she had
ever been when she was five years old... That
moment of naturalness was the crystallising
feather-touch: it shook flirtation into love." (31)*

A whole life here turns on "a feather touch":
elusive, delicate, fine and momentary, its effects
are permanent and damaging. The great irony of
the scene and of the remainder of Lydgate's
unhappy life is that Lydgate should fall for
Rosamond's "naturalness" – an aberration of the
moment in a person who, except on one further
occasion, is studiously, even intrinsically – "she
was by nature an actress of parts" (12) – devoted

to the artificial. The irony is dramatic not sceptical, however, not just because the naturalness *is* natural, involuntarily produced by the play of "minute causes" which has unexpectedly and accidentally placed the couple together in a situation of embarassingly charged physical proximity: the moment is crystallising and definitive because it calls into play aspects of Lydgate which most deeply define him, both as a man – "the ambitious man... was very warm–hearted and rash" (31) – and as a doctor: "he was used to being gentle with the weak and suffering". (31) Not one key or cause, but numerous influences – relating to the past as well as the present, to personal and professional character, to the novel and the known – determine this moment. "In all failures," the narrator says at the opening of this scene, "the beginning is certainly the half of the whole." (31)

But what this passage as a whole suggests is that there is no getting back to a "beginning" or originating cause – a difficulty which is only compounded in view of the fact that Lydgate feels already compromised in this situation by the subtle influence of Middlemarch gossip concerning the supposed understanding between Lydgate and Rosamond: "Momentary speculations as to the possible grounds for Mrs Bulstrode's hints had managed to get woven like slight clinging hairs into the more substantial web of his thoughts." (31) Middlemarch provincial conventionalism is all the more hiddenly pervasive in its effects upon Lydgate for seeming to him so petty and insignificant. Lydgate's situation is an image of the collision and convergence of the many and the various which, in this novel, makes "things severally go on". (31)

"The time was gone by," Dorothea Brooke acknowledges, "for guiding visions and spiritual directors." This novel might well be sceptical about systems but it is not cynical about the human need for them. Rather the narrating voice explicitly recognises that ordinary human life could not for a moment carry on without the kind of belief which accepts them. "Scepticism, as we know, can never be thoroughly applied, else life would come to a standstill: something we must believe in and do." (23) The search for definitive grounds of individual belief, *and* the inevitable dangers or failures of any such quest, are given equivalently urgent and plausible representation, as an example of the obdurate incompatibilities – like that between self and world or self and other – that seem, in this novel's world view, to be built into the system of life.

What does the novel have to say about marriage?

In *Middlemarch*, couples are brought together in marriage only to remain unfulfillingly apart.

One devastating example occurs in Chapter 58, where the financial difficulties experienced by Lydgate and Rosamond reach crisis point.

He laid his hand softly on hers, saying –

"Dear!" with the lingering utterance which affection gives to the word... "I am obliged to tell you what will hurt you, Rosy. But there are things which husband and wife must think of together. I dare say it has occurred to you already that I am short of money."

Lydgate paused; but Rosamond turned her neck and looked at a vase on the mantelpiece.

"...I took pains to keep it from you while you were not well; but now we must think together about it and you must help me."

"What can I do Tertius?" said Rosamond, turning her eyes on him again. That little speech of four words, like so many others in all languages, is capable by varied vocal inflexions of expressing all states of mind from helpless dimness to exhaustive argumentative perception, from the completest self-devoting fellowship to the most neutral aloofness. Rosamond's "thin utterance" threw into the words: "What can I

do!" as much neutrality as they could hold. They fell like a mortal chill on Lydgate's roused tenderness. He did not storm in indignation – he felt too sad a sinking of the heart. And when he spoke again it was more in the tone of a man who forced himself to fulfil a task. (58)

This is the sort of scene F.R. Leavis had in mind when he spoke of "the sensitive precision of George Eliot's hold on dialogue" and the "living tension" she creates with it. Not only every word spoken but every detail of voice and movement is minutely recorded. George Eliot's mind and language is here at its most micro-surgically fine and exact in its analysis of the plenitude of implication in Rosamond's thin utterance. No one could be more superficial, we feel at this moment, than Rosamond. But the narrator's presence here gives a sense of depth and meaning even to Rosamond's lack of deep meaning by showing what that lack itself means to Lydgate, how much he feels her lack of feeling.

The power of this passage and of the entire chapter from which it comes is its patient dramatisation of the "total missing of each another's mental track" (58) which is a tragic central failure of the Lydgate-Rosamond relationship. In obeying the formal requirements of dialogue, moving to and fro from one to the other of this couple, giving equal weight to both sides, the narration reveals that Lydgate, like Rosamond are two separated worlds rather than two halves of a whole one.

Often it is merely the silent gap between paragraphs which signals the immensity of distance between partners who are "together" in life. In the following definitive scene, at the very centre of the novel, the close of Book Four, Chapter 42, Casaubon has just learned from Lydgate that he is dying, and Dorothea goes to join him in the garden. "She might have

THE 'PIER-GLASS'

The novel's most famous scientific analogy occurs in Chapter 27 in relation to Rosamond:

An eminent philosopher among my friends, who can dignify even your ugly furniture by lifting it into the serene light of science, has shown me this pregnant little fact. Your pier-glass or extensive surface of polished steel made to be rubbed by a housemaid, will be minutely and multitudinously scratched in all directions; but place now against it a lighted candle as a centre of illumination, and lo! the scratches will seem to arrange themselves in a fine series of concentric circles round that little sun. It is demonstrable that the scratches are going everywhere impartially, and it is only your candle which produces the flattering illusion of a concentric arrangement, its light falling with an exclusive optical selection. These things are a parable. The scratches are events, and the candle is the represented a heaven-sent angel coming with a promise that the short hours remaining should yet be filled with that faithful love that clings the closer to a comprehended grief":

> *His glance in reply to hers was so chill that she felt her timidity increased; yet she turned and passed her hand through his arm.*
>
> *Mr Casaubon kept his hands behind him and allowed her pliant arm to cling with difficulty against his rigid arm.*

egoism of any person now absent – of Miss Vincy, for example. (27)

While each individual inhabits what seems to him or her to be a "centre" – his or her own consciousness – that centre is in fact "only" (an innocently terrible word in this context) the "flattering illusion" produced by self-absorption. Moreover, that apparent centre, most dizzyingly of all perhaps, is only *one* among infinite possible centres (those of "any" other person) where personal egoism operates to render individually meaningful, events which are intrinsically "impartial" and arbitrary. The use of scientific and religious discourse together in this "parable" suggest that this law is at once ancient and empirically provable: the phenomenon will hold true at every repetition of the experiment. The experimental lives of this novel, moreover, validate that law. The pier-glass example seems to offer, even from within the novel, a non-novelistic, clinically objective explanation of the fates of the characters as creatures subject less to the author's deterministic plot than to necessary human laws. ◆

There was something horrible to Dorothea in the sensation which this unresponsive hardness inflicted upon her. That is a strong word, but not too strong: it is in these acts called trivialities that the seeds of joy are forever wasted... You may ask why, in the name of manliness, Mr Casaubon should have behaved in that way. Consider that his was a mind which shrank from pity... Besides he knew little of Dorothea's sensations, and had not reflected that on such an occasion as the present they were comparable in strength to his own sensibilities about Carp's criticisms. (42)

Again, minute attention, in the first two sentences, to what is going on at the surface level of look and touch, is supported, as the scene develops, by scrupulously incisive disclosure of what exists around or beneath those actions. What the passage as a whole discloses as it imaginatively inhabits now Dorothea's, now Casaubon's experience of the moment, is how these two are inadvertently hurting one another out of the equivalent sense of hurt they are suffering within themselves. Even the effort of sympathy which does go out from Dorothea to Casaubon remains entirely and uselessly separate from him. The initial paragraph division – a Dorothea paragraph, then a Casaubon paragraph – bears silent witness to the fact that neither Dorothea nor Casaubon can cross the boundary of being which separates them as easily as the author-narrator can. Together in marriage, together in the moment, they are doomed to suffer the unhappiness and mutual failure of their relationship alone.

Are these failures simply the result of bad marital choices? Perhaps like many first-time readers of the novel, you felt that the truly compatible partners were Dorothea and Lydgate. Certainly this is one of the novel's many shadow stories, a "might have been". And it is no accident that immediately before his entreaty to Rosamond, Lydgate has recalled Dorothea's voice of "deep-souled womanhood" when he treats her husband's illness:

"Advise me. Think what I can do. He has been labouring all his life and looking forward. He minds about nothing else and I mind about nothing else –"

For years after Lydgate remembered the impression produced in him by this involuntary appeal – this cry from soul to soul, without other consciousness than their moving with kindred spirits in the same embroiled medium, the same troublous fitfully illuminated life. (30)

What truly connects Dorothea and Lydgate here is decisively opposed, in fact, to the largely egoistic "attraction" which has led to their respective marriages. Indeed, the fellowship which begins here is a form of painful, even arduous, kinship which is possible only because of the troubled experience in marriage which they share in common yet must suffer alone. The mutual recognition does not resolve anything, bring relief or make things better, any more than Dorothea's or the narrator's sympathy for Casaubon does any tangible good. In ordinary life a Casaubon would resist the imaginative sympathy the narrator extends as completely as he shuns Dorothea's: "Consider that his was a mind which shrank from pity." In the "real life" of the novel, Lydgate and Dorothea can have no dramatic release from the trouble and pressure of their married life.

Yet it is precisely because these characters are stranded in small lives in a small town without the possibility of direct alleviation that the author feels compelled to register the slight gestures which show humans at their best, in the thick – or rather "shallows" – of life's worst. Dorothea's "Think what I can do" gives Rosamond's little speech of four words ("What can *I* do?") one of those tiny vocal inflections which produce a complete difference of human emotional meaning. Even her unwanted pity is rewarded, though *en passant*, too late and ineffectually, when at the end of Chapter 42, Dorothea resolves to try to ease her husband's suffering, and waits for him as he leaves the library to retire to rest.

"Dorothea!" he said, with a gentle surprise in his tone. "Were you waiting for me?"

"Yes, I did not like to disturb you."

"Come, my dear, come. You are young, and need not to extend your life by watching."

When the kind quiet melancholy of that speech fell on Dorothea's ears, she felt something like the thankfulness that might well up in us if we had narrowly escaped hurting a lamed creature. She put her hand into her husband's, and they went along the broad corridor together. (42)

The final sentence recalls the close of Milton's *Paradise Lost* as Adam and Eve, "hand in hand, with wandering steps and slow", leave Eden. It is a clue to what marriage means in this novel. It is not simply an oppressively wrong institution, outdated and moribund, as it was to be regarded later in the century by Thomas Hardy. Nor is marriage the fulfilment of a Victorian ideal of domestic romance. Rather it is the most intense testing ground for negotiating the tension between self and other, self and world; for suffering the loss of dreams and ideals within the exacting limits of the real; for discovering, paradoxically, the essential loneliness of separated consciousness. Marriage is the place where the innocent dream of life ends and adult reality begins.

How important are work and money in *Middlemarch*?

Dorothea's repeated question – "What could she do, what ought she to do?" (27) – articulates a critical human question for an increasingly secularised era. Its variation recurs repeatedly in the novel – "What shall you do?", "What was he to do?" – as if the question were expressing a state of baffled anxiety susceptible to the whole range of human experiment. In an earlier age, as the Prelude suggests, a Dorothea and her contemporaries might have found fulfilment of her desire to "make her life greatly effective" in a religious calling. In the post-religious era of the mid to late Victorian period, however, the kind of need which Dorothea and her contemporaries express was almost bound to seek fulfilment in the secular activity of work. There is hardly a character in the novel (major or minor) who does not speak for, confront or represent the question of what to do with an individual life as a pressing human issue.

Fred Vincy, for example, has no epic ambition but his situation resonates with Dorothea's, as from major to minor key: "What secular vocation was there for a young man (whose friends could not get him an 'appointment') which was at once gentlemanly, lucrative, and to be followed without special knowledge". (56) As the son of a Middlemarch manufacturer, Fred is "inevitable heir to nothing in particular". (13) In a newly democratic world, traditionally settled hierarchies of rank and status were disappearing or being replaced. As Fred's future prospects rely upon the incalculable generosity of old Mr Featherstone's will, so Will Ladislaw is dependent upon the income provided by his relative, Casaubon. Fred and Will thus represent a whole generation of young men in the early 19th century for whom the choice of career had become an issue because there was no inherited social position to bestow the gift of vocation.

In this respect *Middlemarch* is, as Henry James called it, a mode of "history" indeed. Fred's disappointment over the Featherstone fortune like Will's rejection of first Casaubon's, then Bulstrode's offer of patronage, is an indirect reflection of the historical-economic reality that no one in Middlemarch can evade. In this newly-commercialised English world – increasingly dominated by the middle-classes and by market forces – money (literally "a living") is something to be made or earned rather than to be passed down from one generation to the next. No one can simply opt out of such a world, for commercialism has become the condition in which the individual must survive and which crudely levels and

TEN FACTS
ABOUT MIDDLEMARCH

1

Middlemarch is a blend of two separately conceived stories: "Miss Brooke", and a study of provincial society, entitled *Middlemarch*, centring on Lydgate. "Miss Brooke" came to form the Prelude and the first 9–10 chapters of the completed novel; the original *Middlemarch* became the basis of Chapters 11–16.

2

George Eliot whose greatest novel was *about* failure, was continually oppressed by a sense of her *own* failure. "I do not feel very confident that I can make anything satisfactory out of 'Middlemarch'" she wrote in her journal. After the roaring success of *Adam Bede*, the author had written: "It seems impossible to me that I shall ever write anything so good and true again."

3

Middlemarch was originally published in eight separate instalments, published at roughly two-monthly intervals, each "Book" having its own title and being like a little novel in itself.

4

When *Middlemarch* was published as one volume in 1874, it sold 10,000 copies in six months. The novel's commercial success was briefly repeated in the 1990s when the Penguin paperback reached the top of the bestseller list during the BBC's TV adaptation.

5

The marriage of Ladislaw and Dorothea Brooke takes place at the same time as the passing of the First Reform Bill in June 1832. So Dorothea's embrace of the liberal reformer Will echoes what is happening in Britain as a whole.

6

Although *Middlemarch* belongs firmly in the tradition of English literary realism, in its philosophical bent and profound interest in ideas it is closer to the tendencies of European literature (Goethe, Balzac, Flaubert) in which George Eliot was deeply read.

7

"George Eliot… was a good hater," says a character in A.S. Byatt's *Still Life*. She based Bulstrode on a mid-19th-century preacher whom she hated and, as Marian Evans, stridently criticised in her essay "Evangelical Teaching: Dr Cumming"(1855). She charges Cumming with the worst sectarian excesses (demanding love and charity and fostering hatred) of the Evangelical Christianity to which she had been committed in her own youth.

8.

The model for Caleb Garth was George Eliot's father, Robert Evans, land-agent and manager of the Arbury Estate in Warwickshire where Mary Ann Evans grew up.

9.

Many of George Eliot's letters and journals have been preserved – in particular, her travel journals for the period 1854-65 – and provide evidence of her keen interest in the visual arts. She was invited to a number of artists' studios and private collections, including Dante Gabriel Rossetti's. After eloping with G.H. Lewes, the couple travelled through Germany, recording her experiences of modern German art in a notebook entitled "Recollections of Berlin". She drew upon these years later when describing Dorothea Brooke's honeymoon in *Middlemarch*. Later trips to Italy provided rich material for both *Romola*, and the Rome chapters of *Middlemarch*.

10.
There was a 1994 TV adaptation produced by the BBC in seven episodes, directed by Anthony Page, starring Juliet Aubrey, Rufus Sewell and Douglas Hodge. The mini-series was a hit in Britain, sparking what was described as a "mini-craze for Victorian fiction" (*The New York Times*, Elizabeth Kolbert), including *Middlemarch* lectures, comics and debates.

Caricature of George Eliot, Swinburne and Mark Twain in Cheyne Walk where all three once lived, by John Minnion

"modernises" the historically older virtues embodied in heroic Lydgate, modest Farebrother and the pastoral Garths. Bulstrode's literal financial power over the people of the town is an image of the insidious, pervasive and ineluctable power of money itself in a newly mercantile capitalist age.

At another level, the paralleled situations of Will and Fred offer a paradigm of the anxiety of choice and freedom experienced in a post-traditional society. Like Fred, Will eschews the "inconvenience" of serious application to any one pursuit or specialism in the belief that "the

IMAGES OF SELF

This is a novel full of densely compacted imagery. (See The pier glass, p54.) Windows, mirrors and reflective images abound. Characteristically they express a narcissistic gaze that is turned inward upon the self rather than outward upon the world. (In Dorothea, this distortion or inadequacy of vision is accompanied by her literal short-sightedness.) At one level, for example, the optical image of the pier glass, explicitly targeting Rosamond, draws together disparate examples of egoistic tendencies which precede it in the formal sequencing of the novel:

> *Dorothea had by this time looked deep into the unguaged reservoir of Mr Casaubon's mind, seeing reflected there in vague*

intentions of the universe" will allow him to short-cut the kind of "plodding" perseverance to which Casaubon has committed his life. Compare Fred's own "generous reliance" upon "the favour of providence". (36) But while Fred's answer is to try as far as possible to do "nothing", Will's answer by contrast is to try to do everything – everything that is available at any rate to the embryonic "genius". (10) Given the security of Casaubon's patronage he dabbles promiscuously in the entire range of romantic forms of expression and experience, experimenting with alcohol, asceticism and opium before passing on to a quixotic flirtation with the

---

labyrinthine extension every quality she herself brought. (3)

Fred fancied that he saw to the bottom of his uncle Featherstone's soul, though in reality half what he saw there was no more than the reflection of his own inclinations. (12)

A similar kind of egoism afflicts Mr Casaubon, who is unable to see anything but suppressed rebellion and judgement of his failures even in Dorothea's offers of wifely love. The narrator comments:

Will not a tiny spot very close to our vision blot out the glory of the world, and leave only a margin by which we see the blot? I know no speck as troublesome as self. (46)

In *Middlemarch* almost no major character escapes the moment which as the critic Barbara Hardy has put it "ends the dream of self [and] marks the rude and salutary awakening to the world, where self is reduced". In the case of Casaubon, egoism remains its own punishment. "It is an uneasy lot at best, to be... present at

arts and trying out drawing, poetry, painting and sculpture in turn.

Ladislaw's character is often regarded as idealised but George Eliot arguably goes further in exposing the dangers of Will's dilettantism than the hazards of Fred's initial indolence. The novel continually holds up the comic yet instructively negative example of Mr Brooke, who "like[s] to go into everything" (39), and achieves nothing whatever, as a caricature of what Will himself might become in the continued dispersal of his energies in place of settled commitment to singular pursuit. (Mr Brooke repeatedly sees in

this great spectacle of life and never to be liberated from a small hungry shivering self". (22) The loss of the dream of self in Rosamond and in Bulstrode, by contrast, comes as a terrible Nemesis. When Will Ladislaw makes clear his love for Dorothea in preference to herself, Rosamond "seemed to be waking into some new terrible existence ... she felt a new terrified recoil under a lash never experienced before". (78) When Bulstrode experiences "the quick vision that his life was after all a failure. that he was a dishonoured man" he feels his double-dealing "now turned venomously upon him with the full-grown fang of a discovered lie". (71) In Bulstrode, as in Rosamond, the sense of the world as a malleable extension of self has been absolute. The hard reality which they have refused to see or deliberately evaded now avenges itself upon them, not just toppling the self's supremacy but virtually annihilating any sense of self at all: "[she] was almost losing the sense of her

Ladislaw a younger version of himself. (25) (29) Yet the mistake of choosing the *wrong* vocation is also treated as a hugely serious one in *Middlemarch* even as the novel demonstrates in the stories of Fred and Will – and especially in that of Farebrother perhaps – the extreme difficulty of finding a "fit" between the individual inclination and a settled calling. Economic circumstances forced him to forego a passion for Natural History and enter the clergy. Yet Farebrother's insistence upon the importance of making the right choice of profession suggests that something more significant is at stake than mere

identity" (78); "all this rushed through him like the agony of terror which fails to kill". (71)

The violence of the fall when it comes is a measure of the extent to which, under the terms of this novel's cosmology, Rosamond and Bulstrode need to have forced upon them the knowledge which they will not, or cannot, see for themselves. If the capacity for human fellowship offered for George Eliot, "the humanistic equivalent of, and replacement for, the Christian conception of grace" (as Kerry McSweeney puts it), it follows that the "moral stupidity" exhibited in all her creatures to some degree is analogous to the Christian doctrine of original sin. These moments of awakening in Rosamond and Bulstrode are a secular version of the scourge of the "old Adam". At the same time, they help reveal how Dorothea's "looking out" of her window in Chapter 80 (when she too believes she has been rejected by Will), to a "palpitating life" beyond her own trouble, is, by contrast, a moment of grace. ◆

unhappiness or poverty. When Fred tells Mr Farebrother he "might as well go wrong" by entering the Chruch as any other way, Mr Farebrother remonstrates: "That is nonsense... Men outlive their love, but they don't outlive the consequences of their recklessness." (52) Farebrother raises the possibility that for a 19th-century man the most significant relationship is not that between himself and a woman, mediated by love, but that which exists between himself and the world, mediated by work. In the novel as a whole both "passions" are treated as having equivalent significance.

> *We are not afraid of telling over and over again how a man comes to fall in love with a woman and be wedded to her or else be fatally parted from her... and are comparatively uninterested in that other kind of "makdom and fairnesse" which must be wooed with industrious thought and patient renunciation of small desires? In the story of this passion too, the development varies: sometimes it is the glorious marriage, sometimes frustrations and final parting. (15)*

If the responsibility for choosing the right vocation has shifted to the individual, it is the responsibility of the chosen vocation in part to fulfil the function which used to be assigned to God – that of conferring meaning and individual salvation. From this point of view, work offers the best opportunity a person has in a Godless world for the kind of authentic activity which will satisfy the whole self and redeem a human life from a crushing sense of waste and purposelessness.

In this respect Lydgate, as he himself puts it, is one of the "lucky" ones (16) insofar as the right vocation found him early in life with the force of a religious calling. More, in his ambition to combine his clinical work as a general practitioner with scientific research, Lydgate seeks an identity between his theoretical principles and his practice:

"I should never have been happy in any profession that did not call forth the highest intellectual strain, and yet keep me in good, warm contact with my neighbours. There is nothing like the medical profession for that: one can have the exclusive scientific life that touches the distance and befriend the old fogies in the parish too." (16)

This is a vision of a whole life – one in which the intellectual and the practical, the mental and the physical, the general and the particular, distant and "warm" are all married together. Only Caleb Garth elsewhere in the novel possesses the same certainty in relation to his professional purpose. In fact Lydgate is looking for a version of what Caleb Garth has already found – a calling in which the whole self is perfectly realised. "To do a good day's work and to do it well was the chief part of his happiness" (56); "his virtual divinities were good practical schemes, accurate work, and the faithful completion of undertakings: his prince of darkness was a slack workman". (24) His "happiness" derives from work which is not just an expression of self, but the self's most primary activity.

Caleb, however, belongs to an older, simpler, socially more coherent world, in which conditions existed for the kind of settled and harmonious relationship between man and world which Caleb represents. He is the residual example of an outmoded epic society in which a person is what they do. Where some critics have found sentimental nostalgia in George Eliot's treatment of Caleb Garth, his character seems intended to embody a lost ideal relationship between self and world which no other character in the novel achieves to the same degree. Caleb's success is a measure of everybody else's failure, and a measure too of the problem of finding a simple correspondence between what one is and what one does in an age when, as George Eliot herself put it, "the relation between within and without becomes [every year] more baffling".

Is *Middlemarch* a feminist novel?

"The determining acts" of Dorothea's life, the narrator asserts in the Finale, "were the mixed result of young and noble impulse struggling amid the conditions of an imperfect social state". The conclusion resonates with the Prelude's characterisation of Dorothea, and the idealist young women whom she represents, as "later-born Theresas" whose "blundering lives" are "the offspring of a certain spiritual grandeur ill-matched with the meanness of opportunity". But how far are those imperfections and lack of female opportunity presented as the outcome of a patriarchal social order?

The early books of the novel are awash with heavily-satirised male assumptions about the nature, capacities and role of women in the early books of the novel. For Sir James Chettam a man's mind "always has the advantage of being masculine... and even his ignorance is of a sounder quality" (2) and Sir Borthrop Trumbull asserts that "a man whose life is of any value should always think of his wife as a nurse". (32) Indeed Dorothea's youthful idealism is so sympathetic to the reader at the outset of the novel because she is first introduced via these conventional male banalities:

A young lady of some birth and fortune, who

knelt suddenly down on a brick floor by the side of a sick labourer and prayed fervidly as if she thought herself living in the time of the Apostles – who had strange whims of fasting like a Papist, and of sitting up at night to read old theological books! (1)

The reproachful sarcasm which might be directed at Dorothea's religious fervour is itself ironised here, the more especially because the narrator is impersonating the tone, view and language not of Middlemarch male society in general but of those men who regard themselves as Dorothea's potential suitors:

Such a wife might waken you one fine morning with a new scheme for the application of her income which would interfere with political economy and the keeping of saddle-horses: a man would naturally think twice before he risked himself in such fellowship. (1)

These early minor strains, comic in tenor, are nonetheless echoed in the major plot lines of the novel with tragic issue. Casaubon believes he has found in Dorothea "a modest young lady, with the purely appreciative, unambitious abilities of her sex" (29) while Lydgate imagines Rosamond to be the type of "perfect womanhood ... instructed to the true womanly limit and not a hair's breadth beyond... docile therefore". (36)

Moreover, the two central female characters themselves represent implicit critiques of prevailing cultural and gender stereotypes. Rosamond, at one level, is the most complete victim of patriarchy, since she has in part made herself and in part been made – by her education at Mrs Lemon's school – in the image of conventional male attitudes. She possesses "that combination of correct sentiments, music, dancing, drawing... and perfect blond loveliness... which made the irresistible woman for the doomed man of that date" (27) and she plays the role of ideal woman with the same kind of "executant's instinct" (16) she brings to her piano-playing. Yet it is through Rosamond that George Eliot explodes the contemporary Victorian ideal of womanhood. Rosamond's accomplishments and refinement are achieved at the expense of trivialising her intellect and coarsening her feelings, while her exquisite manner and charm conceal an egoism and social ambition which are the antithesis of the docility she appears to represent.

Dorothea, on the other hand, is no less a victim of the patriarchal order for refusing to conform to its conventional expectations in respect of the role and behaviour of women. The consensus about women's function and capabilities in the community of Middlemarch helps to establish the crampingly oppressive milieu in which Dorothea has to try to forge a life for herself as well as indicating how far her urgent desire to find some activity commensurate with her intellectual and emotional vitality goes against the social grain. If her "slight regard for domestic music and feminine fine art" sets Dorothea apart from Rosamond, still, like Rosamond she finds that her education – "that toy-box history of the world

THE "WOMAN QUESTION"

One key political issue at her own time and throughout the Victorian period was "the woman question". There is no question that George Eliot shared the feminist movement's intolerance of the exclusion of women from educational and professional opportunities as well as its resentment at the inequalities between men and women which were inscribed in legal and political institutions. Not only did she meet some of the most influential campaigners for female rights, Florence Nightingale among them: almost every woman with whom she was close from the 1850s onwards was taking an active part in the women's movement, some of them leading it.

Yet Eliot's support for reform was as cautious as it was ambivalent. At the height of her fame she still refused to take a radical or ideologically partisan stance on the issue of women's rights partly on the grounds of its complexity, and partly out of a belief that pronouncements on the adapted to young ladies" (84) – has unfitted her for anything other than the conventional avenues open to women of her class, those of charitable activity or marriage.

The novel in various ways underscores the degree to which such otherwise distinct women as Rosamond and Dorothea are nonetheless subject to identical socio-cultural pressures. As wives, both feel stifled by the marriages they had looked

woman question did "not come well from" her. Her reluctance publicly and unequivocally to state her position, or to give active and open support to the campaign for female rights, was apparently in part the result of her compromised social position as the partner of George Henry Lewes and a fear, perhaps, that support from a woman who had lost social respect and reputation would endanger rather than promote the female cause. Early feminist criticism of the 1970s was largely hostile to George Eliot, disliking her conservative portrayal of women as embodying the traditional virtues of submission and renunciation. Yet one key

effect of having set her novel back in time is that the female characters George Eliot depicts are even more restricted socially and economically than the women of her own age, so that the frustration of vocational ambition which, in the Prelude to the novel, is described as "the social lot of woman" is brought into sharper focus.

Moreover, the early sections of the novel "get away" with some trenchant satire on patriarchal attitudes to Dorothea which might have been very uncomfortable for her contemporary audience if they had not been distanced by the historical setting of the novel. ◆

forward to, albeit with different hopes and expectations, as offering promise of fulfilment. Rosamond can no more satisfy, through matrimony, her desire for social success than Dorothea can vicariously satisfy her longing for a vocation. The novel seems deliberately to expose the great lie implicit in Victorian ideology that women could fulfil themselves and their needs through marriage and men, while realistically reproducing the conditions whereby women like Rosamond and Dorothea effectively had no "work" but men. The fact that women's very economic survival depends on men entails the ancillary psycho-emotional problem that they have no distraction from domestic infelicity in occupation outside the home. Both Lydgate and Casaubon find solace and relief in professional pursuits or in masculine forms of play (gambling). Rosamond and Dorothea turn instead, as an alternative to the disappointment and frustration of their blighted lives, to another man, and significantly in terms of the structural resonances of the novel to the same man, Will Ladislaw.

Yet for all the quiet subversion of Victorian gender conventions implicit in these relationships, when Dorothea is finally united with Will, her gifts and intelligence are relegated to the role of wifely help to his reforming mission of Member of Parliament. One early reviewer felt that the sense of disappointment elicited by this betrayal of

Dorothea's potential was an aspect of the novel's critique of prevailing structures. "One feels," said R.H. Hutton "*and is probably meant to feel acutely,* that here too, it is the 'meanness of opportunity' and not intrinsic suitability, which determines Dorothea's second comparatively happy marriage". But Dorothea's eventual fate has also been criticised by feminist critics as a symptom of George Eliot's ultimate acquiescence in the oppressive 19th-century ideal of womanhood.

Dorothea is not permitted the radical steps she herself took but, instead, in finally becoming wife, guide and mother, presents renunciation and passivity as ideal virtues. In defence of Dorothea's fate, Kathleen Blake has pointed out that that the opportunities and achievements which marriage to Will opens to Dorothea are not negligible, since his work towards political reform is an undertaking of magnitude: "Dorothea helps forward a movement that would eventually prevail and that bears comparison to Saint Theresa's reform of a religious order as a 'far-resonant' action".

Perhaps to stress or to complain about the novel's feminist credentials is to miss the larger point. As Rosemary Ashton has pointed out, *Middlemarch* is not even "chiefly the drama of a woman's failure", but concerned almost equally [in Lydgate] "with the thwarting of a man's efforts". The novel's inclusive emphasis, implicitly treating men and women as equivalent rather than different, also informs the non-sectarianism of the narrative voice, whose persistent use of "we" effectively collapses gender categories and distances.

Does anyone achieve anything in *Middlemarch?*

In *Middlemarch*, says Alan Mintz, "the rhetoric of social hopefulness is everywhere; one cannot turn a page without reading of notions, schemes, reforms and plans". Talk of model farms, new hospitals, scientific farming, medical improvement, political reform runs throughout the novel and in characters as otherwise diverse as Sir James Chettam and Caleb Garth. It is as if, says Mintz, the "vast and inchoate yearning for the good" which had been initiated by a secular age has been "broken down and distributed among the multitude of fictional forms that populate the novel".

Dorothea is offered as a prototype of this phenomenon. Her own "yearning for the good" is one of the first things we learn about her. In the opening chapters she is drawing up plans for labourers' cottages and, after her engagement to Casaubon, she is disappointed to find that Lowick and its parish does not have a "larger share of the world's miseries..." (9) After Casaubon's death, her philanthropic enterprise, as an alternative to re-marriage, of establishing a "model workers" colony (55) is a utopian project not unlike Will Ladislaw's "intended settlement on a new plan in the Far West", when he feels himself to be "hopelessly divided" from Dorothea. (82)

Dorothea's particular yearnings for "ardent action", and the paternalistic schemes in which they manifest themselves, are determined by the intensity of her own nature, the privilege of her class, and her position as a woman for whom there is no possibility of a settled vocation through which to fulfil and realise her ambition for purposeful life. Yet she speaks movingly for a central and defining experience of the novel when she says to Lydgate in their conversation over the hospital:

> *"How happy you must be, to know things that you feel sure will do great good! I wish I could awake with that knowledge every morning. There seems to be so much trouble taken that one can hardly see the good of!" (44)*

Yet Lydgate's 'trouble' – like that of Bulstrode, Brooke and Ladislaw – eventually comes to nothing. Dorothea's own plans and wide charity meet the obstructed fate of most of the novel's reformist projects. One wonders, said a contemporary reviewer, Edward Dowden, where *anything* is possible. "In this epoch of incoherent ideas and chaotic social forms, heart and brain – Dorothea's sobs after an unattained goodness, and Lydgate's intellectual passion – are alike failures." Later, Marxist critics would complain of a deterministic, even defeatist bias. They protested that this stacking of the fates against the characters' reforming ambitions expressed the author's mechanistic view of society as impervious to attempts by the individual to change it. Certainly the novel offers a salutary check to the liberal dream of progress and presents the latter as a slow, gradual, painful and complex phenomenon on the evolutionary model. Change is the outcome of a constant negotiation between the individual, the social medium in which the latter operates and the larger socio-historical forces which impinge upon both.

Moreover, doing real good in this novel is never a rewarding experience for the individual. In Chapter 80, now believing Rosamond to be her successful rival for Will's love, Dorothea resolves nevertheless to fulfil her promise to Lydgate to visit Rosamond and effect a reconciliation between husband and wife. At this crisis, she herself recognises the contrast between the goodness she had sought to do for others and her "calling" here:

And what sort of crisis might not this be in three lives whose contact with hers laid an obligation on her as if they had been suppliants bearing the sacred branch? The objects of her rescuer were not to be sought out by her fancy; they were chosen for her. She yearned towards the perfect Right, that it might make a throne within her, and rule her errant will. "What should I do – how should I act now, this very day, if I could clutch my own pain, and compel it to silence, and think of those three?" (80)

Dorothea has sought to devote her life-energies to some great project for the benefit of humankind at some vague exotic distance, geographically and temporally, in which her personal influence in the world is writ imaginatively large. Instead her duty turns out to be close at hand, and, more morally surprising still in this novel, these local and apparently modest opportunities for personal heroism require the greatest stamina. The call to goodness which is "chosen for her" is one which Dorothea could not have chosen for herself. Her "fancy" would never have sought, and certainly not at this time and these circumstances, a Rosamond as an "object of rescue". The obligation she feels may relieve her of that terrible Middlemarch burden – "what to *do*" – but only by presenting itself in the form of a responsibility which is almost impossible to be borne.

In fact, all the greatest occasions of doing good in this novel are of a deeply uncongenial and involuntary kind, the sort of calling *no one* would willingly choose. Farebrother intercedes with Mary Garth on Fred's behalf, even though he loves Mary himself; Lydgate supports Bulstrode as he collapses even though this compromises him utterly and destroys his reputation and career. In both cases professional ethics support but do not determine the performance of what is felt to be a human duty. Yet that self-sacrifice is too inconveniently painful and authentically suffered to allow of any of the self-congratulation Dorothea or Lydgate might have imagined would be their reward as foundress of a colony or medical pioneer. There are no egoistic pay-offs here in celebration of noble altruism. This is what "realism" means in this novel, and the novel really exists to bear witness to the achievements which remain thus unrecognised.

Does religion matter in *Middlemarch*?

Middlemarch is a key clue to the disappearance of God in the Victorian period's crisis of religious faith. The 'official' representatives of formal religion render belief either moribund (as in Casaubon), corrupt (as in Bulstrode), or compromised (as in Farebrother, who describes himself in his role as clergyman as "no more than a decent makeshift"). The religion which this novel truly endorses is often grandly titled George Eliot's "religion of humanity", based on the author's translation of Christian principles into a form of secular humanism.

But it is a 'religion' that really has no settled form, calling, or even name. When Will responds to Dorothea's explanation of her personal belief – "desiring what is perfectly good, even when we don't quite know what it is and cannot do what we would" – by calling it "a beautiful mysticism", she says: "Please not to call it by any name... It is my life. I have found it out and cannot part with it."(93) It is this life-evolved, personally authentic religion which the novel really stands by. And for all its informality, it proves far more robust than its counterparts in the novel when Dorothea undergoes the trial which tests it most completely, believing Rosamond Vincy to be Will's lover.

*In that hour she repeated what the merciful eyes
of solitude have looked on for ages in the
spiritual struggles of man – she besought
hardness and coldness and aching weariness to
bring her relief from the mysterious incorporeal
might of her anguish: she lay on the bare floor
and let the night grow cold around her; while her
grand woman's frame was shaken by sobs as if
she had been a despairing child. (80)*

A woman, "discover[ing] her passion to herself in
the unshrinking utterance of despair" admits her
love for a man whom she now believes to love
another. The situation is "not unusual"; the
circumstances are hardly great or heroic. Yet
George Eliot places this struggle unhesitatingly in
a great tradition of the "spiritual struggles of
men"; only the "merciful eyes of solitude" now
replace those of the God.

It is no accident that Dorothea's personally
heroic emergence from despair recalls John
Bunyan's great Christian epic, *A Pilgrim's
Progress*.

*She opened her curtains, and looked out towards
the bit of road that lay in view with fields beyond,
outside the entrance-gates. On the road there
was a man with a bundle on his back and a
woman carrying her baby; in the field she could
see figures moving – perhaps the shepherd with*

his dog. Far off in the bending sky was the pearly
light; and she felt the largeness of the world and
the manifold wakings of men to labour and
endurance. She was a part of that involuntary,
palpitating life, and could neither look out on it
from her luxurious shelter as a mere spectator,
nor hide her eyes in selfish complaining. (80)

The "manifold" "largeness of the world" has no
longer to be "kept up painfully as an inward
vision" (28) as it did when she suffered the
oppressive tightness of her wifely existence. It is
what she sees when she looks out of the window,
where she is herself now a figure in the vision. The
hope which this man and woman seen beneath the
sky give to Dorothea comes not as a blinding
revelation but almost as an egoistic check; if
Dorothea is "a part of that involuntary, palpitating
life", still she is only "a *part*" of it. The vision is
won at the cost of Dorothea's fullest recognition of
her own littleness in relation to the world's
largeness. Her achievement is not sudden
conversion but the finding of a 'middle way'
between two negative extremes ("neither as mere
spectator", "nor in selfish complaining"). This
great moment in the novel embodies an
immanent, as opposed to transcendent, faith – a
belief that humanity's final meaning and hope is to
be found within life not outside or above it. And in
this novel hope comes in unlikely places. When, in

Chapter 74, Mrs Bulstrode has learned of her husband's disgrace, she locks herself in her room.

She needed time to get used to her maimed consciousness, her poor lopped life, before she could walk steadily to the place allotted her... She knew, when she locked her door, that she should unlock it ready to go down to her unhappy husband and espouse his sorrow, and say of his guilt, I will mourn and not reproach. But she needed time to gather up her strength; she needed time to sob out her farewell to all the gladness and pride of her life. When she had resolved to go down, she prepared herself by some little acts which might seem mere folly to a hard onlooker... (74)

In the time-out allowed by the locked room, Mrs Bulstrode finds the strength to commit herself to her "lopped" future life, and even – in embracing humiliation and "espousing" his sorrow – to "re-marry" Bulstrode. What really happens here is a hidden and lonely playing out of the marriage service. Mrs Bulstrode's "little acts" contain within them, subterraneously, very big things. There is nothing merely conventionally dutiful in Mrs Bulstrode's resolve to go down to her husband. It is a brave act of loyalty. But it is a great act performed by an imperfect, rather dull woman who requires the support of small rituals – taking off her ornaments and putting on a plain gown and bonnet "which made her look suddenly like an early Methodist".

The prose recalls this religious aura a paragraph or so later when Mrs Bulstrode approaches her husband and says, "Look up, Nicholas", as if in secular imitation of the Bible's "Look up, and lift up your heads; for your redemption draweth nigh" (Luke 21:28). But in *Middlemarch* there is no redemption. There is forgiveness, but only of a compromised kind. "She could not say, 'How much is only slander and false suspicion?' and he did not say, 'I am innocent.'"

Those words end the chapter in this world of no happy endings. Yet something is achieved here. "There is a forsaking," the narrator remarks early in the passage, "which still sits at the same board and lies on the same couch with the forsaken soul, withering it the more by unloving proximity." This is not a preachy generalisation but a memory: we think of Rosamond's response when Lydgate says they must "think together". "Lydgate paused; but Rosamond turned her neck and looked at a vase on the mantelpiece."(58) It is one of those "acts called trivialities" (42) which gives retrospective meaning to Dorothea's apparently useless gesture in relation to Casaubon: "His glance in reply to hers was so chill that she felt her timidity increased; yet she turned and passed her hand through his arm." (42) The ecology of the novel reclaims such moments, even as they make nothing better, as not merely redundant or wasted but as worthwhile, for holding the promise of something better in human relations. So, too, when Mr and Mrs Bulstrode are brought into one sentence in the final paragraph of the chapter – "He burst out crying and they cried together, she sitting at his side" – what happens helps in its small way to redeem those earlier failures.

What Dorothea cannot do for Casaubon, what Rosamond will not do for Lydgate, Mrs Bulstrode does do for her husband. Mrs Bulstrode is no perfect saviour. She saves her marriage not the world. But even in its very closeness to failure, this patched-up marriage with its near-view of death, preserves a memory of what is possible for the species.

Rufus Sewell and Juliet Aubrey in the BBC's 1994 adaptation

CRITICS ON *MIDDLEMARCH*

"What do I think of Middlemarch? What do I think of glory – except that in a few instances this 'mortal' has already put on immortality. George Eliot is one."
Emily Dickinson, 1873

"If we write novels so, how shall we write history? ... Perception charged with feeling has constantly guided the author's hand, and yet her strokes remain as firm, her curves as free, her whole manner as serenely impersonal, as if, on a small scale, she were emulating the creative wisdom itself." Henry James, 1873

"A magnificent book which, with all its imperfections, is one of the few English novels written for grown-up people." Virginia Woolf, 1919

"Probably no English writer of the time, and certainly no novelist, more fully epitomises the nineteenth century."
Basil Willey, 1949

"No Victorian novel approaches Middlemarch in its width of reference, its intellectual power, or the imperturbable spaciousness of its narrative."
V.S. Pritchett, 1946

"For many writers and many readers, including myself, the thought of 'the novel' in the abstract is followed by Middlemarch in the particular." A.S. Byatt, 1999

Why is the final meeting between Rosamond and Dorothea so important?

In his study of 19th-century ethics and the novel, *The Burdens of Perfection*, Andrew H. Miller argues that 19th-century narrative form embodies a belief in, and model of, moral perfectionism – the capacity to perfect what is distinctly human in us – through "responsive unpredictable engagements with other people".

> Without dispensing with either third-person or first-person perspectives, the novel and moral perfectionism give special weight to second-person reactive perspectives with their I-you-me structure.

The affective dynamic of second-person relations – I to you and back to me – as the basis of moral thinking and behaviour is exhibited most unproblematically perhaps in the work of Jane Austen. Elizabeth Bennet and Mr Darcy, Emma Wodehouse and Mr Knightley, learn to become suitable marriage partners for one another largely through their (albeit initially reluctant) openness to reciprocally corrective example. The affective "success" of second-person relations in *Pride and Prejudice* and *Emma* is in part a consequence of the fact that their prototypical form – conversation – is an aspect of accepted social ritual and decorum, quite as much as is dancing quadrilles or getting married.

In the multiplicity and diversity of *Middlemarch*, even the social norms of marriage and profession are desperately lonely and unhappy affairs, as if in illustration of Matthew Arnold's famous proclamation in *A Study of Poetry* that "the dialogue of the mind with itself" had begun. Moreover, many of the central second-person relations of *Middlemarch* disclose, as we have seen, all that cannot be said, achieved or fulfilled by or within them. In formal terms, *Middlemarch* can seem largely to split – or, as in free indirect mode, to hover – between isolated or egoistic first-person perspectives and the third-person perspective of the narrator which extenuates or redeems such limitation.

Yet, in *Middlemarch*, the morally affective power of second-person relations – the capacity of one person to influence another – is arguably stronger on those occasions when it *is* displayed than in any other 19th-century novel. Indeed, says Miller, in George Eliot's rendering of the ethical life, the knowledge of how and why one should behave "derives... most often from the partialities developed out of relations with particular others." George Eliot's commitment to what her contemporary John Henry Newman called, from a religious perspective, "personal influence" operates in the test of conversation that is more vulnerably intimate than safely "social".

Here is the conversation – written at one sitting, said George Eliot – which takes place between Dorothea and Rosamond in Chapter 81, following Dorothea's resolution in the previous chapter to "clutch [her] own pain" and seek to intervene in what she supposes is a love triangle between Rosamond, Lydgate and Ladislaw. At first, Dorothea hardly knows how to distinguish Rosamond's trouble from her own. "Marriage is so unlike everything else," she begins. "Even if we loved someone else better ... it murders our marriage – and then the marriage stays with us like a murder – and everything else is gone."

Filled with the need to express pitying fellowship rather than rebuke, she put her hands on Rosamond's, and said with more agitated rapidity, – "I know, I know that the feeling may be very dear... it may be like death to part with it – and we are weak – I am weak –"

The waves of her own sorrow, from out of which she was struggling to save another rushed over Dorothea with conquering force. She stopped in speechless agitation, not crying but feeling as if she were being inwardly grappled. Her face had become of a deathlier paleness, her lips trembled, and she pressed her hands helplessly on the hands that lay under them.

Rosamond, taken hold by an emotion stronger than her own – hurried along in a new movement which gave all things some new, awful, undefined aspect – could find no words, but involuntarily she put her lips to Dorothea's forehead which was very near her, and then for a minute the two women clasped one another as if they had been in a shipwreck.

"You are thinking what is not true," said Rosamond, in an eager half-whisper, while she was still feeling Dorothea's arm round her – urged by a mysterious necessity to free herself from something which oppressed her as if it were blood-guiltiness.

They moved apart, looking at each other.

"When you came in yesterday – it was not as you thought," said Rosamond in the same tone... "He was telling me how he loved another woman, that I might know he could never love me," said Rosamond, getting more and more hurried as she went on. (81)

The "mysterious necessity" which compels Rosamond to speak the truth to Dorothea has been characterised as divine grace translated into its human equivalent, intense fellow-feeling. Certainly the novel's generous breadth of vision in thus going beyond rigid categories of egoist and altruist, saved and damned, to show a person acting against the current of their entire life and nature, is testimony to the novel's belief in "a secular version of a Christian paradox"; namely, that even the most self-centred human creatures can contribute to what Kerry McSweeny calls the "humanistic economy of salvation".

Yet the moment is powerfully moving because the prose is assiduously careful to specify the particular human origin, occasion and substance of this "religious" feeling. Indeed, the narration avoids abstract or non-literal language except in order to convey how, for both women, feeling is experienced as an overwhelmingly material, tangible, even painfully physical force – as "waves", "movement" and, later in the chapter, "tumult". For feeling is manifestly communicated, intensified and rendered irresistible through the literal physical closeness of the two women, and by what goes on in silences, at the level of touch or sight. The pressure of Dorothea's hands, of Rosamond's lips, of the latter's "half-whisper" or their mutual clasp gives special significance to their "looking at each other" finally, even as they move "apart". Fellow-feeling is generated and sustained entirely by the intimate overlap and interaction between the two women.

Rosamond had delivered her soul under impulses which she had not known before. She had begun her confession under the subduing influence of Dorothea's emotion... With her usual tendency to over-estimate the good in others, [Dorothea] felt a great outgoing of her heart towards Rosamond for the generous effort which had redeemed her from suffering, not counting that the effort was a reflex of her own energy. (81)

One person's goodness and generosity begets another's which, on the rebound, begets more of the same. The passage shows the dynamics and mechanics of that "mysterious" process by which invisible emotional material given off by one person becomes an active agent in the life and mind of another, in part through its catching that person pre-egoistically and involuntarily, without the usual defences against the power of human feeling.

A species of this "reflex energy" moves Fred Vincy "quite newly" when Mr Farebrother warns Fred – thus sacrificing his own hopes of happiness – that he is on his way to losing Mary's love by slipping into bad (gambling) habits: "A fine act produces a sort of regenerating shudder through the frame and makes one ready to begin a new life. A good deal of that effect was just then present in Fred Vincy."(66)

These triumphs of human fellowship are limited and often temporary. The benevolent unfamiliarity of Dorothea's influence on

Rosamond is swiftly overtaken by narrow resentment at Will's rejection of her, even before her "generous" speech is ended. "He said you would never think well of him again. But now I have told you and he cannot reproach me any more" is a sign that the habitual spoilt child has reasserted itself against the more child-like simplicity of her rush of "serious emotion" toward Dorothea. Yet one of the great realist achievements of this novel is that these small human acts, even as they reveal the highest human virtues, remain caught within the restricted prosaic medium of provincial life, subordinated in situation and circumstance.

If goodness is to survive, it must make its way through such limited opportunities as are on offer. And these passing instances, so small in themselves, gain power and resonance through their cumulative repetition. The same phenomenon repeated across a number of characters begins to take on the character of a general law, discovered at ground level, demonstrating the "saving influence, ... the divine efficacy of rescue that may lie in a self-subduing act of fellowship". (82) These acts help to produce the qualified optimism – "Hope dispersed in fragments" as Barbara Hardy has called it – which is the undertow of the novel.

How does Eliot show the depth of feeling between Dorothea and Will?

The other conversations that are emphatically distinguished from the lonely separateness which characterises the Dorothea–Casaubon and Rosamond–Lydgate dialogues are those which take place between Dorothea and Will Ladislaw. As Gillian Beer says, the series of "interviews" – as George Eliot called them – between Dorothea and Will record the "extent to which falling in love *is* conversation; the passionate discovery and exchange of meanings". Dorothea's attraction to Will "grows through the play of spirit and learning between them: they teach each other. He frees her from desiring martyrdom; she gives him a great project."

Beer's reading is a welcome corrective to the traditional reading of Will as an unworthy partner for Dorothea: the "only eminent failure in the book," said Henry James; "not substantially (everyone agrees) 'there'," said Leavis. The lightness and insubstantiality liberally remarked upon by Will's critics within the novel also – "dilettantish and amateurish" (19), "a very pretty sprig "(34), "a kind of Shelley" (37), "a sort of gypsy" (43) – are inseparable, in fact, from the "unfinished" openness and responsiveness which makes possible, almost uniquely in this book, the mutual sharing of thoughts and meanings between Will and Dorothea, who "educate each other" (Beer). While the childlike qualities, and apparent absence of sensuality, in the Dorothea–Will relationship has embarrassed many critics, it is primarily the conversations between them – and their exceptional character relative to other love relationships – which demonstrate that the "innocence" of their relationship is not simply "romantic" or facile, but delicately earned.

The ease with which adulterous longing might have consumed Will is amply suggested in the sexual potency and near-recklessness of his relationship to Rosamond. His rejection of Rosamond when Dorothea finds them together – "'Don't touch me,' he said, with an utterance like the cut of a lash, darting from her..." (78) – is all the more shocking to Rosamond by its startling contrast with the immediately preceding physical tenderness: "Will, leaning towards her, clasped both her upraised hands in his, and spoke with low-toned fervour." (77) But tenderness turns so readily to cruelty here because of the common origin of both feelings in instinctual desire. The result of his selfish promiscuity, Will fears, in significantly primitive imagistic terms, will be the tightening and squeezing out of those very life-energies ("as with slow pincers" (78)) by the blindly narrow sexual and emotional demands of Rosamond.

The sexual potential of Rosamond's and Will's relationship does not simply contrast with the "idealised" innocence of the Will–Dorothea partnership but offers another of the novel's instructive parallels. In fact, sexuality is by no means merely evaded or displaced in the intimate meetings of Dorothea and Will. After Casaubon's death, their wonted communicativeness becomes involuntarily inhibited by the embarrassed mutual consciousness of the codicil to Casaubon's will, which acts as proxy acknowledgement of the sexual tension between them. "Neither of them knew how it was, but neither of them spoke. She gave her hand for a moment, and then they went to sit down near the window, she on one settee and he on another opposite." (54) "Each was looking at the other, and consciousness was overflowed by something that suppressed utterance." (62) This tension is the tissue of their final climactic scene together, where the "conversation" is only barely verbal. True intimacy occurs in the interstices between explicit utterance. "The door was opened and she saw Will before her."

She did not move and he came towards her with more doubt and timidity in his face than she had ever seen before. He was in a state of uncertainty which made him afraid lest some look or word of his should condemn him to a new distance from her; and Dorothea was afraid of her own

emotion. She looked as if there were a spell upon
her, keeping her motionless and hindering her
from unclasping her hands, while some intense
grave yearning was imprisoned within her eyes.
Seeing that she did not put out her hand as
usual, Will paused a yard from her and said,
with embarrassment, "I am so grateful to you for
seeing me."

"I wanted to see you," said Dorothea, having
no other words at command.

They stood silent, not looking at each other,
but looking at the evergreens which were being
tossed, and were showing the pale underside of
their leaves against the blackening sky. Will
never enjoyed the prospect of a storm so much: it
delivered him from the necessity of going away.
Leaves and little branches were hurled about,
and the thunder was getting nearer. The light
was more and more sombre, but there came a
flash of lightning which made them start and
look at each other, and then smile. Dorothea
began to say what she had been thinking of.
"That was a wrong thing for you to say, that you
would have nothing to try for. If we had lost our
own chief good, other people's good would
remain, and that is worth trying for." (83)

In the first paragraph, Will and Dorothea are as
much subject to the difficulties of understanding
between two people as any couple in the novel,

and the author is as scrupulous in her attention here to every detail of look and movement. For words are nearer to potential wounds or death-blows, than loving gestures ("afraid lest... some word of his should condemn him to a new distance from her"). They are a crude sign of separateness where the finer instinct intuits the opposite, something closer to loving amendment of an essential human loneliness. The lightning flash – like the "electric shock" which Will experiences on unexpectedly meeting Dorothea at Freshitt Hall at the opening of Chapter 39 – is a sign of a dynamic convergence in living being, a kind of birth, which is kin more to creation itself, than to sexuality merely. The Will–Dorothea relationship depicts a union that *includes* sexuality, with especial implicit power, while starting from and going beyond its narrow egoism. "Love" is not distinguishable here from what Dorothea calls "good" and its "worth" is at once tested and re-affirmed in her union with Will.

Is *Middlemarch* the greatest English realist novel?

"To the impatient question, But what do you *mean* by realism?, it is tempting just to lift the novel high and say, I mean This," says Karen Chase. Many of our common-sense or shorthand definitions of "realism" are essentially derived from what George Eliot's novels do. "Ordinary" individual lives are observed and presented, in minutely careful and exact detail, in relation to social and material conditions which are continuous in complex ways with personal psychology.

THE FINALE

It is the Finale which ultimately cuts the characters down to size, not only by rounding off their relatively undistinguished fates but by "placing and framing" the characters and their world in a distant and historically superseded past. The characters, their ambitions, the town itself – each thought they were everything and now... Yet the web image in the first paragraph – "the fragment of a life, however typical, is not the sample of an even web" – suggests an opening out and extension of the lives depicted beyond the scope or reach of the novel. Moreover, the famous opening sentence of the Finale – "Every limit is a beginning as well as an ending" – attests to the

Lydgate's story is one of the best examples of the "realistically" reciprocal influence of self and world in this novel.

> *Lydgate was aware that his concessions to Rosamond were often little more than the lapse of slackening resolution, the creeping paralysis apt to seize an enthusiasm which is out of adjustment to a constant portion of our lives. And on Lydgate's enthusiasm there was constantly pressing not a simple weight of sorrow, but the biting presence of a petty degrading care, such as casts the blight of irony over all higher effort... Lydgate was in debt; and*

author-narrator's sense of the degree to which the formal closure of her characters' lives is a necessary fiction.

At one level, the very heightened formality of the Prelude and Finale in a work of loosely structured realism signposts the inherently artificial nature of fictional beginning and endings. For a novel like *Middlemarch* belongs emphatically to the middle of life. Its principal concern is neither with the Romantic anticipations of childhood nor the drama of death but that part of life in which the individual is most tested by, and more often than not hemmed in by the pressing demands and commitments of ordinary domestic and professional life. George Eliot found beginnings and endings "troublesome", she said, perhaps because they seemed so arbitrary to the writer whose humane realism drew her to the mess, strain and struggle that goes on in the undramatic midst of life, not at its extremes.◆

he could not succeed in keeping out of his mind for long together that he was every day getting deeper into that swamp, which tempts men towards it with such a pretty covering of flowers and verdure. It is wonderful how soon a man gets up to his chin there – in a condition in which, in spite of himself, he is forced to think chiefly of release, though he had a scheme of the universe in his soul. (58)

The passage witnesses how the petty social forces which lie outside of self turn gradually, almost visibly, into what is inside – into character . The "slackening resolution" which produces Lydgate's concessions to Rosamond is the knock-on effect of Lydgate's sense that he is getting deeper into a worsening situation which there is no point in trying any longer to control. The "creeping paralysis" is the result of his appalled recognition of the massive disproportion, in terms both of size and power, between the grandeur of his ambitions and the pettiness of the external frustrations. For the smallness without – "the biting presence", the petty yet desperate necessity to get out of financial debt – is not only incommensurate with but threatening to overwhelm the largeness within, the "higher effort", the soul's "scheme of the universe". But aren't these problems all Lydgate's own fault for his untimely and mistaken marriage to the wrong woman?

James Sully, a contemporary psychologist and friend of George Eliot, said of the author's stories that, looked at from one point of view, they are the "outcome" of her characters'; looked at from another point of view, they are the "formation" of these characters.

The point is not whether Lydgate should have been better, though he might have been, or that society should have been more accommodating, though it could have been. The point is that this novel holds together, in solution as it were, all the forces – heredity, education, social class, historical location, professions and so on – which constantly act and react upon one another in any ordinary human life. Lydgate's story is both the formation *and* the outcome of his character as his life shapes itself, tragically enough, through the interplay of his self and his situation.

This delicate balance of pressures is explicitly evident in the novel's pronouncements on the relation of individual to circumstance. On the one hand, "It always remains true that if we had been greater, circumstance would have been less strong against us" (58). On the other hand, "There is no creature whose inward being is so strong that it is not greatly determined by what lies outside it" (Finale). The emphasis shifts, not mechanically or arbitrarily, but in imitation of the richly fluid interchange and constant dynamic flux between self and world.

But for all its painstaking homage to the powerful influence of an external social world, *Middlemarch* is one of the greatest examples of *psychological* realism. The 20th-century novelist D.H. Lawrence said George Eliot was the first novelist to put all the action on the inside. Henry James's *The Portrait of a Lady*, for example – which "place[s] the centre of the subject in the young woman's own consciousness" and "show[s] what an "exciting" inward life may do for the person leading it" – is unthinkable without the example of penetrative analytical insight set by George Eliot. Indeed, critics have long compared George Eliot's ambition and endeavour as a novelist with those of Lydgate as a scientific biologist, seeking to "reveal subtle actions inaccessible by any sort of lens, but tracked in that outer darkness through long pathways of necessary sequence":

> *He wanted to pierce the obscurity of those minute processes which prepare human misery and joy, those invisible thoroughfares which are the first lurking-places of anguish, mania, and crime, that delicate poise and transition which determine the growth of happy or unhappy consciousness. (16)*

Here is Bulstrode, in the dead of night, keeping watch over Raffles (his blackmailer) with strict instructions from Lydgate as to the sick man's treatment:

> *Whatever prayers he might lift up, whatever statements he might inwardly make of this man's wretched spiritual condition, and the duty he himself was under to submit to the punishment divinely appointed for him rather than to wish for evil to another – through all this effort to condense words into a solid mental state there pierced and spread with irresistible vividness the images of the events he desired. And in the train of these images came their apology. He could not but see the death of Raffles, and see in it his own deliverance. What was the removal of this wretched creature? He was impenitent – but were not public criminals impenitent? – yet the law decided on their fate. Should providence in this case award death, there was no sin in contemplating death as the desirable issue – if he kept his hands from hastening it – if he scrupulously did what was prescribed. (70)*

What makes desire so powerful here is that it is experienced not as thought, idea or word but as an image or perception: "He could not but *see* the death of Raffles..."; "... there spread with irresistible vividness the *images* of the events he desired". Here George Eliot discovers the "first lurking place" of "crime" in all its direct sensuous primacy. Yet the "scientific" pursuit of first causes is never morally neutral in *Middlemarch*. The point at which Bulstrode sees "his own deliverance" is the secular equivalent in this novel of the moment of the Fall. When free indirect mode emerges in this instance – "What was the removal of this wretched creature?" – it is to mimic Bulstrode's internalisation of the devil's own voice.

Its immediate moral consequence comes in the next knock-on sentence: "In the train of those images came their apology." As soon as the desired end dictates the decision, so soon does Bulstrode have to banish the moral, thinking part of himself, and even put reason distortedly in the service of the realisation of his desire: "Should Providence in this case award death... Even here there might be a mistake; human prescriptions were fallible things." When Bulstrode's reasoning faculty is thus used to justify his own wrong-doing he has effectively jettisoned the critical intelligence that could prevent that wrong-doing. And almost as immediately that critical intelligence comes retributively back, in those "yet"/"if"/"but" clauses which ensue: "Yet the law decided... "; "if he scrupulously did what was prescribed"; "But of course intention was everything..." The complexity exists not for its own sake here but to register with minute exactitude the subtle actions of the (morally distorting) thinking mind in time. The

Ink-on-paper caricature of George Eliot (Gary Brown)

very precision of the language gives it the status of a kind of mental primary "tissue": that "Yet... if... if... but" sequence is the very syntax of moral conflict, the deep grammar of inwardly avenging conscience.

The fact that the grand narrative of sin and temptation now takes place in a private subterranean realm where guilt is its own punishment in the absence of an avenging God, helps explain the very inception of the psychological novel. And George Eliot, its greatest pioneer, shows here the supreme moral stamina involved in imaginatively inhabiting the "invisible thoroughfares" of a mind.

GEORGE ELIOT:

a philosophical novelist

A.S. Byatt has said that as a novelist of ideas George Eliot has "no real heir" in England. "She was European, not little English, her roots were Dante, Goethe, Shakespeare, Balzac." Eliot's reading in philosophy was as deep and disciplined as it was wide-ranging in every sense, going far beyond English national and intellectual limits and extending to the leading movements and ideas of her time.

It was in part through her editorial role (as Marian Evans) at the *Westminster Review,* that George Eliot came into contact with the work of many of the most important intellectuals in Britain and Europe. These included the German philosopher, Arthur Schopenhauer, who was to exert a powerful influence on Eliot's contemporaries, Leo Tolstoy and Thomas Hardy, in the final third of the 19th century.

In Schopenhauer's major work, *The World as Will and Idea* (1818), the will to live is the central principle of the universe, appearing in the whole of nature, animate and inanimate alike. The apparent separateness of the individual human will is merely an illusion since "the striving after existence is what occupies all living things and maintains them in motion".

The first task of humans, said Schopenhauer, is survival.

But when existence is assured, then they know not what to do with it; thus the second thing that sets them in motion is to get free from the burden of existence, to make it cease to be felt, "to kill time", i.e. to escape from ennui. Accordingly we see that almost all men who are secure from want and care, now that at last they have thrown off all other burdens, become a burden to themselves.

The impossibility of finding anything that makes survival worthwhile was Hardy's despair. "What was he [Jude] reserved for?" asks Jude the Obscure when even his attempt to commit suicide is defeated. Schopenhauer's vision was thus entirely in tune with Hardy's late 19th-century pessimism which rendered existence merely secondary and redundant, without primary or essential meaning.

Tolstoy's novels are also filled with characters who suffer from a sense of the purposelessness of life. ("Only not to see *it*, that dreadful *it*" as Pierre Bezhokov exasperatedly puts it in *War and Peace.*) But Schopenhauer's "solution" to the "will to life" problem resonates as much as does the problem itself in Tolstoyan fiction. If it is the intensity of will which causes suffering, says Schopenhauer, it follows that the less humans exercise will, the less they will suffer. Moreover, once the will or ego is surrendered, the distinction between one human and another disappears, and the identity of all creation is truly apprehended. Perhaps the most Schopenhaurean moment in the whole of 19th-century fiction is the death of Prince Andrew in Tolstoy's *War and Peace*, when, after his fatal wounding at the Battle of Borodino, he sees at the ambulance station the man who has been his bitter rival in love and "Remember[s] the connection that existed between himself and this man who was dimly gazing at him through tears that filled his swollen eyes":

> *He remembered everything and ecstatic pity and love for that man overflowed his happy heart.*
> *Prince Andrew could no longer restrain himself, and wept tender loving tears for his fellow men, for himself, and for his own and their errors. (book 3, ch 37)*

This is no mere formal act of forgiveness – rather a deeply involuntary recognition that between himself and this other human creature the likenesses are greater than the differences even as they are opposed to one another in life. Prince Andrew's death is a moving, particularised instance of the Schopenhauerean dictum that life is a sleep, a dream, an illusion and death an awakening.

George Eliot's own work, especially her aesthetic of sympathy, overlaps with Schopenhauer's insofar as the recognition of others as "equivalent centres" of human meaning is identified with an emergence from "moral egoism". (21) But George Eliot, like Tolstoy himself in *Anna Karenina*, wanted the loss of ego as an ethical possibility within life and not only at the dramatic climax of near-death. The starkly contrasting fates of Dorothea Casaubon and Anna Karenina are instructive here. While the seeming cause of Anna's ultimate suicide is the sexual jealousy she feels in relation to her lover, Vronsky, the true cause, in Schopenhaurean terms, is, paradoxically, not a sacrifice of life and will, as in Prince Andrew, but only the most despairing and defeated expression of the "will to live" ego*istically*, for oneself alone. When, by contrast, Dorothea, overcomes her jealousy to act on her rival Rosamond's behalf, she achieves the new relation to self and others not "too late", at the point of death, but in the relatively banal situation of a small provincial town where, even so, it can do some genuine good.

> *All the active thought with which she had before been presenting to herself the trials of Lydgate's lot, and this marriage union which, like her own, seemed to have its hidden as well as evident troubles – all this vivid sympathetic experience returned to her now as a power: it asserted itself as acquired knowledge asserts itself and will not let us see as we saw in the day of our ignorance. She said to her own irremediable grief, that it should make her more helpful, instead of driving her back from effort. (80)*

But in Schopenhauer's thinking, "compassion" is apparently no more ethically motivated than the philosophical system of which it was a part. The overwhelming pessimism of this did not appeal to George Eliot the meliorist. Dorothea's sympathetic "power" at this juncture resonates more closely, in fact, with the thinking of those philosophers whose work

George Eliot (as Marian Evans) translated into English – Ludwig Feuerbach's *The Essence of Christianity* (1841 trans. 1854) and Baruch de Spinoza's *Ethics*. Though belonging to different centuries and distinct cosmologies (one broadly religious, the other broadly humanist), these thinkers had the common appeal to George Eliot of affirming that an individual's acknowledgement of limitation was a first step to overcoming it and thus to making possible connection to others. Love, for Feuerbach, made possible the apprehension of species-life which only death can achieve in Schopenhauer. For Spinoza, the requisite power was reason. While the fullest truths lay beyond the perception of human limitation, still to own one's finitude is better to understand one's nature. Central to Spinoza's thinking was the idea that irrational egoistic passion or negative emotion could be countered only with an even stronger positive emotion brought about by reasoning and intellectual effort: subduing of the passions could be accomplished not by pure reason alone but by reason-induced emotion.

GEORGE ELIOT

and the 19th century novel

Middlemarch is a definitively mid-19th century novel, standing between the moral assurance of pre-Victorian Jane Austen, on the one hand, and the fin de siècle evolutionary pessimism of Thomas Hardy on the other.

George Eliot's letters and journals show she was a keen reader of Austen's work, and not infrequently her irony in *Middlemarch* is tonally close to Jane Austen's, especially when it is used to expose provincial society's predatory instincts. Compare the opening of *Mansfield Park* (1814) - 'There certainly are not so many men of large fortune in the world as there are pretty women to deserve them' – with Chapter 35 of *Middlemarch*, on the reading of old Peter Featherstone's will: "These nearest of kin were naturally impressed with the unreasonable expectations in cousins and second cousins, and used their arithmetic in reckoning the large sums that small legacies might amount to, if there were too many of them."

But, aside from their shared, adroit comic irony, the two novelists were very different. In Austen's world, says Tony Tanner in his introduction to the Penguin *Pride and Prejudice*, a bad marital decision can be a momentous event, threatening a pre-existent pattern and order in which private morality and social good are ethically inter-related aspects of one another. Austen's world still largely possesses and rests upon the "coherent social faith" which George Eliot, in her Prelude to *Middlemarch* four decades later, mourns the loss of for the 19th century, where laissez-faire individualism and secularisation had replaced the part-Classical, part-Christian social morality of an earlier age.

When, for example, Fanny Price, heroine of *Mansfield Park*, refuses to marry Henry Crawford because she recognises in his polished propriety and elegant charm a counterfeit morality, she embodies Jane Austen's resistance to the danger posed by moral dissimulation in a modern social world. Yet the refusal - even from this plain, quiet heroine - cannot happen without social notice and rupture.

In Austen's world, morality is never truly private - as it is, in *Middlemarch*, for Mary Garth, when she refuses old Featherstone's request to burn his most recent will (which, it transpires, excludes Fred, her childhood sweetheart, from the old miser's inheritance) or for Dorothea when Casaubon asks her unconditionally to carry out his wishes in the event of his death. In both cases, a young woman is urged to submit to pressure as peremptory as it is compromising from men who - as employer and husband respectively - hold the balance of power. Yet, for all the novel's silent sense, in these parallels, of a shared moral struggle, each woman is entirely and terrifyingly alone - in the dead of night, at the climactic point of near-death - with her own particularised instance of it.

In fact, when Dorothea goes to make known to her husband her brave commitment to accede to his wishes, he is already dead. Her struggle is not only profoundly lonely, but entirely too late. But for George Eliot these moral tests were worth enduring and passing even if no-one ever knew they had happened or what they had cost. In the late Victorian fiction of Thomas Hardy, by contrast, the inward life which suffers loneliness in *Middlemarch* has become utterly and finally alienated, even redundant, in the protagonists of *Tess of the D'Urbervilles* and *The Mayor of Casterbridge*. For the world would not care about that inner life, even if it knew of its struggles: "She was not an existence, an experience, a passion, a structure of sensations, to anybody but herself. To all humankind besides Tess was only a passing thought." (*Tess of the D'Urbervilles*, 1891, ch. 14)

Moreover, in a meaningless world, the protagonists themselves have ceased to care. When Elizabeth-Jane, to whom Michael Henchard has falsely claimed a paternal relation out of despair of losing her, accuses Henchard of deceiving both herself and her real father, Henchard finds he "did not sufficiently value himself to lessen his sufferings by strenuous appeal or elaborate argument". (*The Mayor of Casterbridge*, 1886, ch. 44) Hardy himself could not "sufficiently value" suffering or failure to conclude that they were worth the painful human cost.

George Eliot had much more in common with Hardy than with Austen. A novelist of regional life, like Eliot, Hardy had also lost his religious belief; his novels, like George Eliot's, bore the inflection (and, in Hardy's case, burden) of the intellectual and scientific advancements of the age. Hardy's men and women are set against an impersonal and indifferent natural or cosmic process which drives them toward their biological destiny in crass disregard of their emotional and spiritual needs.

Yet Hardy's characteristic narrowing of the generous social width of *Middlemarch*, forcing a single protagonist, as in *Jude the Obscure*, through a repetitively defeating plot whose one sure forward momentum is toward the end of death, leaves no room for the compensating relations which the formal openness of George Eliot's "particular web" makes possible. In the range, richness and expansiveness of character and situation of *Middlemarch*, even the loneliness which characters suffer individually creates a sense of community and hidden, diffuse connection and contribution to "the growing good of the world". For Hardy, failure is simply failure. There is no consolation in a world which has lost the coherent religious context that promised salvation.

Where Hardy never got over the loss of the coherent metaphysic which underwrites Jane Austen's work, George Eliot set her novels to do what good they could in a world increasingly losing its way. Yet despite this many early readers complained of her melancholy and pessimism and agreed with Sydney Colvin's assessment that the novel leaves us emotionally unsatisfied, "sad and hungry". The fact that *Middlemarch* is finally tonally closer to Hardy than to Austen – as though George Eliot just missed being Hardy – is itself a measure of the novel's formal achievement. Jane Austen's moral point of view and the form of her novels coincide, says Alasdair MacIntyre in *After Virtue*. "Jane Austen writes comedy rather than tragedy for the same reason that Dante did; she is a Christian and sees the telos of human life implicit in its everyday form." George Eliot's realism holds the middle-ground between Austen comedy and Hardyesque tragedy, believing neither in the prior existence of telos or purpose, nor in the impossibility of finding meanings adequate to sustain a human life.

1819, Nov 22 George Eliot born Mary Ann Evans, 22 November, South Farm, Arbury, Warwickshire.

1836 Mother dies. Takes over charge of household. Learns Italian, German Greek and Latin.

1842 Refuses to attend Church with father: finally agrees to join him to spare his feelings.

1851 Moves to London. Assists John Chapman with editorship of the *Westminster Review*.

1854 Leaves England with George Henry Lewes, who is unable to obtain a divorce from his wife. Relationship cuts her off from her family. Publishes translation of Ludwig Feuerbach's radical challenge to orthodox belief, *The Essence of Christianity*.

1858 Now living with Lewes in Richmond, publishes *Scenes of Clerical Life,* 'Amos Barton', under pseudonym 'George Eliot'.

1859 *Adam Bede,* which sells 16,000 copies in first year.

1860 *The Mill on the Floss*. Travels with Lewes to Italy.

1861 Publishes *Silas Marner*.

1862 Offered astounding sum of £10,000 for new novel (*Romola*), by publisher Smith and Elder.

1866 *Felix Holt* published but not a commercial success.

1869 Begins *Middlemarch* (the 'Lydgate' portion).

1870 Abandons *Middlemarch* believing it to be a failure.

Embarks on a new story, 'Miss Brooke'.

1871 Combines the two stories. *Middlemarch* begins serial publication in eight parts.

1876 Last novel, *Daniel Deronda,* begins serialised publication.

1878 Lewes dies. George Eliot goes into seclusion.

1879 Begins to see John Cross, who is 20 years her junior and a close friend of Lewes's.

1880 Marries Cross and moves to Cheyne Walk. Brother Isaac writes to congratulate his sister after refusing to communicate for almost 25 years. Dies December 22 and is buried at Highgate Cemetery.

BIBLIOGRAPHY

Rosemary Ashton *George Eliot*, Oxford University Press, 1983

Dorothea Barrett, *Vocation and Desire: George Eliot's Heroines*, Routledge, 1989

Gillian Beer, *George Eliot. Key Women Writers*, Harvester Wheatsheaf, 1986; *Darwin's Plots: Evolutionary Narrative in Darwin, George Eliot and Nineteenth-Century Fiction*, Routledge and Kegan Paul, 1983

Kathleen Blake, *Love and the Woman Question in Victorian Literature: The Art of Self-Postponement,* Barnes & Noble, 1983

A.S. Byatt and Nicholas Warren, eds., *George Eliot: Selected Essays, Poems and Other Writings*, Penguin Books Ltd, 1990.

A.S. Byatt, *Passions of the Mind: Selected Writings*, Chatto & Windus, 1991

David Carroll ed., *George Eliot: The Critical Heritage*, Routledge and Kegan Paul, 1971

Karen Chase, *George Eliot: Middlemarch*, Cambridge University Press, 1991; *Middlemarch in the 21st Century*, Oxford University Press, 2006

J.W. Cross Ed., *George Eliot's Life as Related in her Letters and Journals*, 3 vols, Edinburgh: Blackwood, 1885.

Philip Davis, *The Victorians. The Oxford English Literary History, Vol.* 8, 1830–1880, Oxford University Press, 2002

Elizabeth Deeds Ermarth, *Realism and Consensus in the English Novel*, Princeton University Press, 1983

Gordon S. Haight, ed., *The George Eliot Letters*, 9 vols, Yale University Press, 1954-78; *A Century of George Eliot Criticism*, Houghton Mifflin, 1965

Barbara Hardy, *The Novels of George Eliot: A Study in Form*, Athlone Press, 1959; ed., *Middlemarch: Critical Approaches to the Novel,* Oxford University Press, 1967; Ed., *Critical Essays on George Eliot*, Routledge & Kegan Paul, 1970.

Margaret Harris and Judith Johnston eds., *The Journals of George Eliot*, Cambridge University Press, 1998

W. J. Harvey, *The Art of George Eliot*, Oxford University Press, 1962

U. C. Knoepflmacher, *Religious Humanism and the Victorian Novel: George Eliot, Walter Pater and Samuel Butler,* Princeton University Press, 1965

F.R. Leavis, *The Great Tradition*, Chatto and Windus, 1973

George Levine, ed., *The Cambridge Companion to George Eliot*, Cambridge University Press, 2001

Ian MacKillop and Alison Platt, '"Beholding in a Magic Panorama": Television and the Illustration of *Middlemarch*' in Robert Giddings and Erica Sheen, eds., *The Classic Novel from Page to Screen*, St Martin's Press, 200.

Kerry McSweeney, *Middlemarch*, Allen and Unwin (1984)

Andrew H. Miller (2008) *The Burdens of Perfection: On Ethics and Reading in Nineteenth-Century British Literature*, London: Chatto & Windus, 1991

Alan Mintz, *George Eliot and the Novel of Vocation*, Harvard University Press, 1978

Bernard Paris, *Experiments in Life: George Eliot's Quest for Values*, Wayne State University Press, 1965

Ruby Redinger, *George Eliot: The Emergent Self*, Bodley Head, 1976

John Rignall, eds., *Oxford Reader's Companion to George Eliot*, Oxford University Press, 2000

INDEX

First published in 2012 by
Connell Guides
Spye Arch House
Spye Park
Lacock
Chippenham
Wiltshire SN15 2PR

10 9 8 7 6 5 4 3 2 1

Picture credits:
p.9 © Alamy
p.41 © Moviestore collection Ltd / Alamy
p.65 © Corbis
p.90 © Rex
p.111 © Bridgeman

A CIP catalogue record for this book is available from the British Library.
ISBN 978-1-907776-07-6

Assistant Editor: Katie Sanderson
Typesetting: Katrina ffiske
Design © Nathan Burton
Printed in Great Britain by Butler Tanner and Dennis

www.connellguides.com